D1202700

# Witches In A
# Crumbling
# Empire

# Witches In A Crumbling Empire

*Rhyd Wildermuth*

GODS&RADICALS PRESS

This work CC-BY-NA 2018
Rhyd Wildermuth

First Printing 2018

ISBN: 978-1-7325523-0-2
Published by Gods&Radicals Press
PO BOX 11850
Olympia, WA, 98508

Direct all inquiries to the above address,
or email us at
Distro@abeautifulresistance.com

# *Within*

**-To-**

Eijra, for whom all I am was forged.
And to the Harrower, the Liberator, the Crown of the North, the Raven
King, the Lady of Springs and Flames, the Wanderer,
and all whom led me here to you.
And to Peter & Alkistis.

# PRELUDE

At Samhain I saw a vision, the echoes of dreams now resounding again as words: we will all rush to save what is dying, but death will not be denied. Fear, panicked breath as the pain courses through our bodies undulled by all the opiates of forgetting.

We have drugged ourselves for a very long time, we in the cities and suburbs of the Empire. Drunk on cheap oil, high on the rush of glowing screens, fitting for the next new hit of cheap labor to fill our stores. But now the bottle's empty, the baggy turned-inside-out-empty.

Sobering is not fun. Coming off heroin too fast can kill you, few ever escape meth. The more glorious the feeling, the more exuberant the high, the more the bowels rend from its loss. Gay men who've used crystal will tell you this, "no sex seems good without it." A lover escaping heroin told me, "you never know how much life is pain until dope shows you what it could be instead."

I've done neither, but I've held a man who cried while he thumb-scrolled his phone looking for a recovery meeting. I've held a man sweating and shaking all night, urging on the early-morning trip to the methadone clinic. It is like this, watching those around us panic.

They weren't counting the bottles, didn't know they had no other pack and the store was closed. Some of them crawl along the carpet or try to pick out electoral challenges that might have fallen between the cushions. "We didn't vote for him" we hear, but like what comes from the hardest addicts came also the blame. "It was Russia, the third-parties, voter-fraud. You dropped some, I saw you. Call that guy you don't like, I'll let him do me too if he's got black tar."

Empire is dying. The opiates have run out, the distractions don't work any longer. Even as many around us still fight off the tremens, more than we could have dared imagine are gazing upon the horror that had been industrial, Capitalist civilization with sober eyes. Too many heat waves, too many droughts, too many forest fires choking the air of cities to ignore any longer.

You are reading these words because you've noticed, too.

While Empire may have thought it could cheat death, it is we who have learned to become it. We who wait with ash-darkened blades unglinting in crescent moonlight. Assassins, all of us, biding our time in community gardens, stirring cauldrons in soup kitchens, learning spells from books of theory and histories forgotten. Long nights of meetings around tables or in trance with comrades living, dead, or in-between.

We have chosen to endure pain rather than trade time for empty wealth, chosen to endure cold in draughty basement apartments or suffocation in crowded shared houses rather than sell time to Capital. We have declined the easy out, refused to look away at the images of bombs and the charts of lowered water tables. We have chilled ourselves in rain, risking arrest to stop strangers from getting killed. We have listened to the panic of the earth rather than the assurances of the priests. We have known this Empire could not last, and we refused to pretend otherwise.

It is our time.

The works collected in this book, comprising two years of poems, prose, and theory, are for those of us who have refused to look away from what is coming, and those of us who have danced to hasten this fall.

I offer these words to you as love letters and as warnings against fear and false answers.

The wild abandon of a lover and the chill ocean off the Gulf of Morbihund in Bretagne woke the realization that became **Excuses. Marys of the Sea** weaves tales of the revolutionary dead I've met together with the cults of the mari-morgans, including Arianrhod who seems to be the queen of both.

**The Spectre of the Whore** explores the Nazi and Liberal Democrat obsession with the katechon and its enemy, Babylon. **What They Don't Tell You About Vulnerability** and **The Trade** are both love letters: you do not need to endure everything, only what can be made beautiful.

The next two pieces are also love letters, but to the land. **Paganism**™ is one of my most-read pieces, a manifesto for those of us who know that the truths we've seen cannot be bought or sold. **It All Tastes of Sorrow** is a reminder that our relationship to land (just like any relationship) will never be always joy.

Sex kills you, kills what needs to die, and sex is a powerful antidote to the dehumanizing commodification of our bodies and selves into the Capitalist machine. **Gift of Crow, Gift of Stag** is about sex, and also about death, and about what comes after.

**Magic Waiting Beneath Running Feet** is for everyone who hears the screams of what is coming in the echoes of what was, the panic and fear of war and slaughter that comes when Empire seeks blood for its altars. **Bastard Children of a Slaughtering Empire** tells the dark story of the Chalagawtha and the Appalachian Mountains where I was born, land and people raped to build all those things too many of us accept as societal "good."

**Change** is a love poem to the person woven through many of these works. **That Feeling Again, Mr. Frog** is about the time just before the hope of love.

The next three wrestle with the absurdity of social media. **The Summoning** tells of the end of the hope of love and asks who the "self" in a "selfie" really is. **The Hunger of the Feed** was written after a friend tried to kill herself "live" on social media. **A New Luddite Rebellion** invokes the loom-breakers and their spectral captain in a manifesto against mediated existence.

The falling debris of Empire leaves clouds of dust that obscure vision. For some, the temptation to fall back upon simple answers, cheap promises of normality, and easy dichotomies is irresistible. The next four essays are written against those on both the Right and the Left who urge others to do the same.

**Awakening Against What's Awakened** and **The World Without Forms** both give serious attention to Carl Jung's famous "Wotan" speech while critiquing both the rush to authoritarianism by the Right and the dangerous dismissal of esoteric philosophers by the Left.

**Good White Men** criticizes the reduction of political identities to genitals and skin color, a reduction that only feeds the agenda of white nationalists and Fascists. **Barbarians in the Age of Mechanical Reproduction** is a much longer analysis of this problem through a critique of the writings and aesthetic of Jack Donovan ("easily the best critical analysis of what we're doing that I have read," he said in a comment when it first appeared on Gods&Radicals).

**Witches in a Crumbling Empire**, the major essay after which this collection was named, was first presented as a speech to a packed room at a Pagan conference, and this is the first time it has appeared in print.

**Like Water** and **I Told You I Have Always Known You** are again about love. So is the final piece, **The Flood**, written when a dead friend made a visit to run around the forests of my head to make sure I knew what the forests outside my head were saying.

Nothing coming will be easy. None of the crises or calamities befalling this Order of Meaning will leave us untouched. Worse will always be coming: more extinctions, more storms, more heat waves, food shortages, water crises, collapsing infrastructure, and many more wars. Nowhere will be safe from any of this, and the only way out will be through.

I hope these words keep you in hope. Not hope that things will get better, nor that things can be the same again; instead, the hope that comes when one has stared at the death of something that must end and smiled.

Be always well.

Midsummer, 2018
Rennes, Bretagne

# *Excuses*

I am trying to collect all my favorite images of you. But already, there are so many that they run together like the images of a film or the flow of a river. To pull any one image out I would need to stop the film, to stop a current, to ignore all the images before and all the images after which together make you.

Still, though it is impossible, an image I would hold forever is the way you threw yourself into the frigid waves of the sea.

It surprised me: I was afraid you were cold. You said you were cold.

I was cold.

I had decided I would not go under the water, and because you said you would not go under the water, I could have an excuse.

I have too often needed excuses for what I really want to do but don't. Like throw myself into the world, throw myself into love, or throw myself into crashing waves on a beach where 15 years ago I stood in that water, asking myself if I was dreaming.

Now I know that dreams and life and time and love are not like rivers, but like the sea. Now I know that time doesn't move only forward, anymore than waves do. Time surges and recedes in the grand movements of tides, but also in the uncountable moments of waves advancing towards you and then away.

# *Excuses*

And so now I know the answer to that question. Yes, I was in a dream, but one I'd not yet dreamt, one which 15 years later I would dream as I watched my excuses ebb from me as you threw yourself into that sea.

When you stood shivering I had my excuse. When you plunged face first into the cold I watched my excuses slip away from me forever.

Ask me another time and I will tell you the image I most want to remember is the flower you so seriously put in my nose as the sun set atop that sacred mountain. You are so serious when you play—so serious when you dive into water too cold for the hundreds of others wearing wetsuits around us, so serious when you dump wet clay-sand into my hair and scrub it into my scalp, so serious when you laugh riding my back out of a forest as owls call to your soul.

Ask me another time and I will maybe tell you it is those images, not this one.

But ask me now and I will say it again: your body, shaking in love for yourself against the chill of the sea, all your fur wet and matted, and afterward your eyes meeting mine, still saying to me: *we no longer need excuses.*

# Marys of
# the Sea

*O Maria, bela Maria pijèrni mi…*
I catch a glimpse of myself in a mirror and I'm not here.

Everything's gone sepia, the music from the speakers no longer digital but analogue. Pale gauze curtains sweep across the window in wind turned autumnal.

I stare at my reflection. I'm thinner, younger. The white shirt I'm not wearing is stained but pressed, suspenders holding up trousers sized from when I consumed more than coffee and cigarettes.

He's not me. But he's me, and we're listening together to the music, to the silent stairwell outside the door, waiting for footsteps.

The wind has swept away lingering haze, leaving behind taut anxiety, a body tensed to flee, a mind knowing there's nowhere to go. He thinks of his friends, I think of my friends. We, together, shake off the sorrow with a brief turn of the head.

We sigh together, and wait.

*In your garden is a serpent; make wine from it and give it to him.*
Trudging slowly across hot streets in a searing Mediterranean sun, the song rose up. So estranged from the others around me and worried, it felt

like an old friend. "Maria, beautiful Maria," they sang as I shielded my eyes against the unkind light.

He and I remembering this together, across decades. The others marched off not to the sea but to ashes. I'd heard an echo of his sorrow along those dry, cobbled streets; maybe he'd heard my echo just then, staring at his haggard but beautiful reflection.

I wonder if he got tired like I did when we stood together. Or did I only feel his fatigue across the years? What did he hear, if not the same song as I?

Now more tired than before, I wish to sleep. But he, sepia-stained, awaits there to speak to me.

It took me awhile to notice him as I fucked another, the curtains brushing against our skin like fingers, until the man with flesh turned around.

"I like when you do that," he said.

"That was the wind," I answered, happy.

*War has killed so many of your children, O Maria, beautiful Sea.*

There's a cave somewhere along the southern coast of Spain where a man and his sister lived. Beautiful beyond words, he was said to make imperial oracles fall silent when he passed. He was beheaded, his sister perforated with arrows.

I met him in Toulouse, but not him exactly. In a crypt of the Basilica is said to be a piece of his body, encased in a sculpted bust. A line of red paint across his neck reminds the pilgrim that sharpened steel severed his visage from his virile form, but listening long enough it's clear the bone inside belonged to someone else.

"Come with me for awhile," I said to him, and he did.

He was a Cathar, I think. I remember the dream just before, when he and I followed those we thought were friends into some cellar. They were friends, but then weren't. They bound and tortured us. I've been carrying his last screams with me, where they ripped open his bowels and he finally, mercifully, bled out.

There by the Way of the Bull, underneath the Road of the Three Foxes, there's an ancient temple disinterred and filled in. Saturnine, likewise, would cause oracles to fall silent, and he was dragged to ragged flesh across that street before his death. The Basilica is his, they said, but we know what came before that Basilica, and whose rites were celebrated there.

Empire's a long charade of shifting stories. Before I met him (or is it them? The dead are not easy to count), I descended a mountain into Catalonia. I didn't remember him meeting me at the base, but he's there now, again stained sepia with starry dark shadows lingering just past what eyes take in.

He's there with me when I kneel.

*Your husband will come back from the fields and be thirsty, O Maria, bella Maria.*

The dead just don't go away, do they?

He lives in a small house in a village 800 years old in the region known as the Uckermarck. Poland's a minute drive east, Berlin an hour and a half train ride south.

He lives there, and I'm there, visiting. "I bet you smell good," he wrote to me. "I'm not in Berlin much, though—maybe you'd come visit me on my farm?"

"Some people get aroused by sex dungeons and poppers," I replied, brutally excited. "But farms make me hard."

I lied a bit. They don't actually arouse me, but they do fascinate me. Farms in ancient Pagan villages, particularly.

"Come see me." He said. "If you're feeling poorish, I'll buy your ticket."

The train is full. I stand, but on another train I sat. I'm thinking of him, who sat across from me from one village to the next three years before. Wolfish, his work clothes stained, our knees touching, my eyes averting.

We sat this way almost an hour. I'd look up and he met my gaze. I don't think his grey-blue eyes had ever turned away: only mine had, but we didn't need eyes to talk, nor words.

He stood at the door as the train slowed, two hours from Berlin. I raised my head, chanced a glance. He smiled, nodded, and waved as he left, and smiled again that night, his hand choking my throat.

"I'll show you how to use this," he said. We were wolves, his jaw cutting off my air. Arousal turned the fear to desire.

"This is how you use this," he said, his cock trapped in my body, hooked as I awoke to an empty bed.

I'm on this train to an ancient Heathen village, one of the last to fall in Pomerania to the new princes and their empire. Another man meets me at the station; he sniffs me, and I him.

He's not the other, nor is he the man who choked me later, shocked how long I did not need to breathe as stars pierced the sky above us. He could not give enough, and Arianrhod laughed as she wheeled, sharing our little secret.

*Les Saintes Maries de la mer, we will dance your ring.*

I'm collecting the dead, the dead are collecting me. Their secrets and mine are each others, rebels across thresholds of grave dust and living ash.

Wearing a crown of stars and lake-soaked boots I was fucked by a mountain and seeded with fire. Waking in a tomb opened to a city, I laughed, aroused.

Perhaps the dead are of her court, and he's the bridge to her island. These dead, at least.

We'd cross a bridge where Nazis died, and my friend and I both felt them. The urge to jump maddened until I talked to the river, happy to have her tale heard. Upstream's an ancient necropolis, rain washing the dust of the dead to the sea where another waits. From the sea their mist rises, rains down again upon the world, and we are soaked.

The dead come when you come, their breath erotic raising them when you rise.

None of this seems odd any longer, though I understand little.

I understand little, except that sex is the only death we don't go into alone.

# The Spectre of the Whore

## I.

*One must be able to name the katechon for every epoch of the last 1,948 years. The place has never been empty, or else we would no longer exist.*

*–Carl Schmitt, Nazi Jurist*

In ancient Western myths, a certain story persists. It seems to cross cultural and language boundaries, retold by Celts on the far northwestern shores of France and the Greeks bordering the edge of what we now call Europe. Its persistence suggests it to be a core myth of European society; in each version the motifs are the same, the circumstances not much varied, and the consequences deadly.

The story is this: a great, peaceful island, a walled city full of splendor, a paradise. Outside is chaos, poverty, war. Within, perfection, the height of learning, streets full of wealth and happiness. And then, a flood, a storm, a catastrophe.

This place is called by many names: Atlantis, Ys, Cantre'r Gwaelod, Lyonesse. Historians and archaeologists have tried to find evidence of its existence; new-agers have constructed elaborate theories naming it the origin of all occult and magical knowledge. Because its story haunts the lore of so many peoples, perhaps the better question is not "did it exist?" but rather "why do we still tell this story?"

In many of the tales, the great civilization disappears under the sea, and in an unsurprising number of them, this catastrophe is triggered by a woman. I say unsurprising not because women have a tendency to drown cities, but because women tend to get blamed for the downfall of civilization very often. Pandora had her box, Eve her forbidden fruit, and of course, there's the Whore of Babylon.

In the Celtic stories of the drowned island, a woman causes the end by leaving a floodgate open. The Bretons tell it with the daughter of a sea-witch, Dahut; in the Welsh tales, a "well-maiden" named Mererid is the cause. While the misogyny of such tales seems quite obvious, we'd make a mistake if we dismiss these myths as mere propaganda against women and their "weakness." In all these stories, women held in their hands the key to ending what men had built, and in most of them, it was their refusal to obey the order of men which ended one era and began another.

We tend to dismiss such stories immediately as being part of the tapestry of patriarchal terror sustaining our current era. They certainly help uphold this order, but we should not ignore them completely: they tell us something not just about patriarchy, but something deeper about how very fragile political orders actually are. They rely on our obedience.

While we often think of obedience and disobedience as passive stances, the roots and primary usage of the words both refer to action:

*Obey: late 13c., from Old French obeir "obey, be obedient, do one's duty" (12c.), from Latin obedire, oboedire "obey, be subject, serve; pay attention to, give ear."*

That is, an obedient person does what they are told, does their duty, pays attention, serves, becomes subservient to the will of others. There is no passivity implied: obedience and disobedience are both actions.

While women are blamed in every one of these tales for the downfall of civilization, it isn't just their woman-ness which causes these catastrophes: it's their act of disobedience, their conscious withdrawal, their refusal to sustain the current order.

Patriarchal myths do not just blame women for the end of the world, they *feminize* disobedience. Men are good, obedient servants; women are lawless, unruly, disobedient rebels. Doing one's duty, in this conception, is a male trait; rebellion is the nature of women. But in none of these cases is that act of rebellion "passive." It is an active choice which destroys the Garden, opens the box, floods the world.

As most Marxist-feminists (and a few non-Marxist ones) often point out, the patriarchal oppression of women harms both women and men. If obedience and doing one's duty are seen as masculine traits, it's not hard to see why so much government propaganda towards soldiers emphasizes masculinity. A man dies a bloody, painful death on the battlefield because it's his duty to do so. By being obedient to the powers above him, he is being a man: only a woman (or an "effeminate" man) would disobey the will of the leaders.

Thus, to liberate women from this dichotomy is also to liberate men; both are equally bound into the same order of exploitation, just as, according to both Frantz Fanon and James Baldwin, whites are also imprisoned by the creation of Blackness.

To reach this liberation, we must summon the Spectre of the Whore.

## II.

In the final chapters of the Bible a figure appears, astride a horned beast, sitting upon the seas, reigning "over the kings of the earth." Upon her forehead is written:

*MYSTERY, BABYLON THE GREAT, THE MOTHER OF HARLOTS AND ABOMINATIONS OF THE EARTH.*

Peter Grey's book *The Red Goddess* convincingly shows her to be Inanna-Ishtar, the great goddess of Babylon, literally a mother of "harlots" (the temple prostitutes). The continuation of female-led religious groups (particularly embracing a "rebellious" sexuality) was a consistent threat to the early Christian order: no doubt the writer of Revelations intended to invoke such a goddess when depicting the enemy of Christ during the Apocalypse.

While many non-Christian myths similarly named a woman as the cause of civilization's end, Christianity pinning the world's end on a Whore is particularly interesting. A Whore isn't just a woman, it's a sort of woman: not just disobedient, but sexually empowered and liberated. Unlike the other cataclysms catalysed by a disobedient woman, the Christian Apocalypse is reigned over by the mother of whores, of women who are the very embodiment of lawlessness.

The Whore stands outside the patriarchy: she has no husband, so has no one to obey. She also disobeys the natural-political order: sex with her is pleasure and trade, but not for production (of children: i.e., new workers, new political subjects). She demands payment for her services, rather than giving without getting back. And most of all, unlike the dutiful wife, she can refuse.

If the Christians were so certain that their reign could be ended by a Whore, and if our goal were merely the end of codified Christian doctrine, then any heretic should take her seriously. However, we're not just about the end of overt Christianity, but rather the end of the entire capitalist order. The Whore is still a danger, but to understand why, we need to look at how what we think of as "secular" Liberal Democracy is also a continuation and expansion of Christian Empire, and why the Whore still haunts us to this day.

## III.

When religious conservatives in Europe and North America describe their countries as "Christian nations," they usually mean something quite superficial. However, they are not actually wrong, they merely don't go far back enough in history to understand the truth of this.

Christianity started as a religion antagonistic to the Roman Empire, but it did not stay that way. The conversion of Constantine and the adoption of Christianity as the new state religion made certain of this, but we miss something crucial if we leave the story there. Christianity was initially described not as a religion, but as a *disciplina*, a mode of living, control, and governance. Christianity was not just a set of personal beliefs: it functioned also as a political order, with priests and bishops handing down proclamations about right action, warnings against heresy, and specific directions to the faithful below them. When Christianity became the official religion of Rome, this hierarchy increased, especially as bishops became the new oracles of the Empire.

While Pagan Rome was certainly brutal and authoritarian, Pagan state religion only worked well in areas of the Empire where the gods were similar enough to be merged. Much more difficult were the far-flung provinces where ancient beliefs were not so easily assimilated. By the time Constantine made Christianity the official religion of the Empire, Rome had been facing crises of governance, revolts, and an economic panic as its expansion stopped. Christianity's monotheism was an ideal solution to these crises. Not only did it displace a myriad of gods with one totalized God, it also had a coherent moral code, an easily-transferred hierarchy, and an intense missionary zeal.

While it's common to blame Christianity for the fall of the Roman Empire, this is hardly a majority opinion amongst historians. More so, it misses the continuation of Roman imperialism past the official fall of the Empire in 476 through the Catholic Church.

Understand: when a state fails, it doesn't just disappear. Consider what might happen to New York City or Paris if there were suddenly no United States or France; they'd continue, albeit more chaotically. Also, the political and economic influence of those cities wouldn't just go away. When the Roman Empire fell, Rome didn't fall with it, nor did Christianity. They just both lost access to vast legions of soldiers to enforce their will throughout the rest of Europe. This meant they had to find other ways of influencing those around them.

These other means of influence can only be understood through the framework of hegemony, a political arrangement in which a very strong power exerts influence over weaker powers. This influence can be direct or subtle, but it is only sometimes openly violent. Hegemony functions indirectly: other powers do the will of the hegemonic power often without being asked. In essence, they internalize the will of the stronger power and obey it.

The United States is a good example of a hegemonic power. Though it directly rules over only the land it occupies in North America, it exerts political control over the entire western hemisphere because of its military, economic, and cultural strength. South American countries generally do what the United States wants them to do because they implicitly understand the consequences of disobedience. The United States has helped overthrow several South and Central American governments through the CIA, attempted repeated assassinations of leaders like Castro, and has funded antigovernment rebels (the Contras, for instance). Likewise, US-funded propaganda programs (Voice of America, etc.) also ensure complicity, while the vast American media companies help make other peoples more sympathetic to the United States. Thus, to act against the United States is to court death, but no one needs to be told this. America's will becomes theirs.

While this hegemonic influence might appear to be a new aspect of the modern state, Catholic control over Europe after the fall of the Roman Empire functioned in exactly the same way. Consider the propagandistic nature of Church doctrine. Each town and village with a church had a branch-office of this propaganda machine; priests functioned as agents of the Church, ensuring doctrinal uniformity throughout the lands. Through such a network, the Church could exert social and cultural control over the opinions of the people without ever lifting a blade.

Control over the cultural and social forms of societies is control over the people, and it's easy to see why Christianity was so ideal. A religious order which teaches obedience as godly and disobedience as sinful, and one which especially limits and subjugates rebellion in the form of women (whores, witches) perfectly complements political order.

With this control over Christian society, the Church also exerted hegemonic control over monarchies. A king who chose to go against the Pope faced excommunication, revolt from his subjects, and even a crusade from other kings. Without a standing army, the Pope's will shaped the fates of every kingdom around him.

The European political order was a Christian political order. In eight hundred CE, Charlemagne declared the birth of a new Holy Roman Empire, and was crowned Emperor by the pope. This fully wed the Church and the political powers together, a marriage that didn't seem to end until the Reformation. The Reformation and the Enlightenment supposedly meant the end of hegemonic Christian Empire and the beginning of a secular era in European politics. It also meant the birth of Liberal Democracy.

Did Liberal Democracy really escape its Christian predecessors? We can ignore the facile claims of fundamentalists in the United States that America is a "Christian nation." Likewise too easy is the persistence of nominal Christianity within political parties in Europe (for instance, Angela Merkel is a "Christian Social Democrat"). A much stronger case can be made.

The continued Christian nature of Liberal Democracy is seen best by looking at its most staunchly non-Christian advocates: atheist intellectuals. Atheists such as Christopher Hitchens (dead), Stephen Pinker, Richard Dawkins, and Sam Harris have all made extensive defenses of Liberal Democracy and outlined its crucial secular nature. Likewise, all four greatly criticize(d) "intrusions" of Christian morality into secular society. And all four wrote extensively about the danger of one particular religion to Western (secular) civilization.

That religion? Islam, not Christianity. Why Islam? Obviously, it's monotheist, patriarchal, and like all religions has a dangerous strain of fundamentalism. But their obsession with Islam rather than Christianity reveals the persistence of Christian hegemony even in their atheism. Islam is so dangerous precisely because it is not European—that is, it is not Christian.

In the Middle Ages, the Church could (and often did) prevent wars between European states on the basis that they were both Christian. The cultural power the Pope wielded over the people was formidable: few soldiers would want to risk eternal damnation or excommunication for very little pay. Tacit support by the Church (sometimes by taking sides, mostly by remaining silent) was crucial for wars.

The people who were always fair game, however, were Muslims and Pagans. For instance, the wars which eventually forced the last Pagan king of Europe to convert (fourteenth century) were crusades. Likewise, the Reconquista in Spain and all the many crusades into Jerusalem were not just sanctioned but rewarded by the Church. Killing a Muslim was not just okay, it was a holy act, while killing another Christian was murder or worse. Western Liberal Democracies didn't change this. One need only recall that one of the primary justifications for the European Union was that it would keep European countries from warring with each other. Replace the word "Liberal Democratic" with "Christian," and it's not hard to understand why the United States doesn't attack Canada or France. Not only are they not enemies, but they are part of the same community of believers, the new Catholic (universal) communion.

This communion extends not just to their lack of military conflict, but to their united front against Muslim nations. Just as Catholic hegemony acted as a strong barrier against European wars and legitimized wars against Muslims and Pagans, Liberal Democracy legitimizes wars in the Middle East. Not only legitimizes, but mythologizes and glorifies: the invasions of Afghanistan and Iraq in the last decade were done to defend Western Civilization (Democracy, Freedom, "our way of life") just as the crusades were declared to protect Christendom.

That such violence against non-Christians occurs in the name of secularism rather than in Christianity hardly changes anything: in fact, it gives us a clue to what is actually meant by "secular." Consider the bans on Muslim practices in Europe in the name of secularism. Banning hijabs and burkas in the name of protecting women certainly sounds enlightened. However, controlling what women wear, regardless of what it is they are wearing, is still control of women. Likewise, in the name of the secularist idea of "animal welfare," halal and kosher butchery have been banned in at least one European country and several more have tried to follow suit. Yet European methods of butchery (factory farming, industrialized slaughterhouses) can hardly be called humane and are not up for discussion. Consider, too, Switzerland's ban of minarets, France's ban on religious symbols (but not crosses) in public schools, and the "war on terror" (including Trump's plans to deport Muslims): these are even more examples of how Liberal Democracy continues to function as a Christian political order.

While the word "Christian" can be used interchangeably with "Liberal Democracy," we cannot end this history of Empire here. Other words equally suffice and are just as important. One of those words? White. When Canada, the United States, Germany, the United Kingdom, Australia, and New Zealand all committed troops together to fight the civilizational threat of Islamic Terrorism, only white people could have missed the fact that it was an alliance of powerful white nations against Arabs. Within those countries, fear and hatred of immigrants is likewise racialized.

There's a tendency to chalk all of these wars without and within Liberal Democratic nations up to "white supremacy." This is an accurate—but incredibly incomplete—understanding. Whiteness is powerful, and whites are absolutely dominant in white Liberal Democracies. However, whiteness is merely a mechanic, a formula which helps determine whether or not someone belongs. That is, the hegemonic political order called Liberal Democracy is white, but whiteness is the effect of that order, not the cause. Whiteness developed only recently, and only as a way of determining privilege within Liberal Democracies (whites on top) and undermining allegiances amongst the lower-classes which threatened the entire political order.

Likewise, Liberal Democracy is patriarchal, but this is again a function and governing method of the order. Women absolutely receive fewer rights, fewer protections, less wealth, less political power, and endure more violence than men. This is unquestionable. However, fighting the patriarchy is not enough to destroy Liberal Democracy. It is accurate but inadequate to describe our current order as patriarchal, just as fighting white supremacy only attacks the method of governance, not governance itself.

We can string together litanies for days on what Liberal Democracy is (bell hooks, for instance, uses the term "Imperialist White-Supremacist Capitalist Patriarchy," which is much too short) and doing so can certainly help us understand how thorough its hegemonic control is. By calling it Liberal Democracy, we must mean all the strands of the kyriarchal web while remembering that the entire web must be destroyed, not just one strand.

So here we are now, governed by a hegemonic political-theology simultaneously Christian, European, imperialist, patriarchal, white, capitalist, etc. It is all-powerful, soaking through every one of our social, cultural, economic, and political interactions. We are flies in its web, trapped, breaking one strand yet caught by even more in our struggle.

24

## IV.

Though Liberal Democracy officially denies its Christian nature, a very minor text within the New Testament managed to form the basis for its entire political strategy:

*And you know what is now restraining him, so that he may be revealed when his time comes. For the mystery of lawlessness is already at work, but only until the one who now restrains it is removed.*

*– 2 Thessalonians 2:6-7*

The author (Paul) is writing to members of the new order he is building, warning them not to act like the end-times are at hand. Before the Antichrist (the "he/him" to which he refers) can arrive, "what is now restraining" and "the one who now restrains"( Greek: *katechon*) must be removed. Meanwhile, the "mystery of lawlessness" (Greek: *anomia*: being outside the law, wicked, or unruled) is already at work.

Regardless of what Paul actually meant by this section (there are countless theories), the concept of something holding back the chaos and lawlessness of the end-times persists to this day.

Consider the most recent election in the United States. The Democratic Party offered a pro-capitalist centrist candidate with deep ties to corporate oil, finance, and banking industries. Despite her obvious allegiance with the very things which are currently destroying the earth, many on "the left" supported her anyway, seeing her as the only chance to restrain the pure violence of a Trump presidency. That is, Hillary Clinton was presented as the Katechon, the only way to hold back a terrifying flood of wickedness and chaos.

In the United Kingdom, the same arguments were used to justify remaining as part of the European Union. Center-left activists particularly were terrified of what might come were the United Kingdom to leave. Loss of protections, the end of mobility, increasing domestic violence, erosions of wealth all would come if Brexit occurred. In this case, the European Union was the Katechon, the only thing holding back the flood of misery and poverty.

The Katechon is seen also in questions of terrorism, security, and international war. The terrorist is *anomia*, the lawless/wicked ones, currently at work undermining civilization. The sense of "unruled" and "lawless" is particularly relevant: the terrorist obeys no government and operates outside the moral order of Liberal Democratic societies. The terrorist doesn't work within Liberal Democratic "law," seeking justice through the courts or change through electoral politics. Rather, the terrorist blows things up.

Here, shutting down borders, removing rights and protections, increasing surveillance, arresting dissidents, and waging foreign wars is what holds back the flood. None of this really works though, since any individual might "spontaneously" become a terrorist, given the right circumstances. Still, these actions are increasingly implemented in the name of holding back the chaos, keeping the enemies outside the gates, holding back a surging tide. That is, the Katechon.

This is the very same logic which prevents revolution in Liberal Democratic societies. Talk of ending Capitalism, disarming the police, or even all-out revolt is dismissed by evoking the fear of what might happen without those things. Without the police, there would be only *anomia*, lawlessness. Who would protect us from foreign enemies if we had no governments and military? How would we get our medicines, food, and electricity without Capitalism?

This is not just a contemporary trick of Liberal Democracy. The same logic operated in Hobbes' conception that life outside the strong state would be "nasty, brutish, and short," in the checks on popular democracy (including the electoral college) written into the United States constitution, in the Terror which followed the French Revolution, and in all the formations of other states throughout the nineteenth and twentieth centuries.

Both right-wing and left-wing ideologies fell victim to the cult of the Katechon: Marxism's shift to a statist ideology through Trotsky, Lenin, and Stalin was a response to the fear of *anomia*, while it was Fascist theorists who most openly spoke directly about the Katechon: Oswald Spengler and Julius Evola both sought to stave off a coming Apocalypse through an embrace of ancient imperial forms, and the Nazi jurist Carl Schmitt (quoted at the beginning of this essay) saw Hitler as the Katechon, the last hope of civilization against lawlessness and disorder. From his diary:

*"I believe in the katechon: it is for me the only possible way to understand Christian history and to find it meaningful."*

This begs a question: If the leading jurist for the Nazi regime was so intent on having a Katechon who could hold back the tides of chaos, what great evil could possibly have been worse than the gassing of ten million people? Is the lawlessness, the "Antichrist" that the Katechon restrains, really all that worse than the brutality of our current political orders?

## V.

The Katechon exists to hold back a coming catastrophe. In the earliest iteration of it from Paul, the Katechon restrains the revelation of the Antichrist; it holds back the Apocalypse.

Fear of the Apocalypse is a significant part of most Evangelical Christian sects. On the extreme end are the relentless predictions, the certainty that Jesus is about to return and will judge all the nations of the world, leading to some fascinating and frightful behaviors. The Apocalypse, though, isn't confined to devout Christians waiting for the rapture or a literal horn-blowing angel. Nor do I just mean the libertarian Mad Max or Walking Dead fantasists. Governments, too, are terrified of their own end and what might come after.

What is an Apocalypse really, except the end of one order and the beginning of the next? And here's where we should remember what the word apokálypsis actually means. The last book of the Bible in most English editions is called "Revelations," but its older name is "Apocalypse." Both words mean the same thing, hidden knowledge unveiled. The Katechon holds back the Apocalypse and restrains a revelation against the "mystery of lawlessness," holding back the tides of chaos by keeping something hidden.

What's the Katechon hiding? What doesn't it want us to see? What knowledge must it hide from us lest the Whore and the Antichrist walk the earth?

Liberal Democracy is destroying the planet: warming the oceans, melting the ice caps, extinguishing species, poisoning the water. Industrialisation increases this damage, alienating us from one another, turns us into machines. Liberal Democracies wage war on defenseless peoples in foreign countries, kill minorities, trample the poor, and exalt the rich. They keep women oppressed, rape the earth, and sell nature back to us as packaged trinkets to be thrown away back into the open wounds of that great Whore Earth.

Yet all the while, we cling tightly to it. We cannot end Liberal Democracy, because worse will come. What could be worse? The Katechon whispers, "You need me. I am holding back the Antichrist. I restrain the Whore. I am preventing the Apocalypse. You will die without me."

Though the Bible ends with the Whore of Babylon, it begins with the very first Whore, the very first lawless one. Everyone living under Liberal Democracy knows her name, knows that Whore's crime. You can't escape it, you cannot avoid knowing how she destroyed everything.

She, too, heard the warnings of the Katechon.

She heard what would happen if she did not obey, heard the consequences of disobedience.

She also heard something else:

*"You will not certainly die," the serpent said to the woman. "For God knows that when you eat from it your eyes will be opened, and you will be like God, knowing good and evil."*

*– Genesis 3:1–4*

At the beginning of this essay I asked why these stories of women destroying the world are told. By now, you must already know the answer. And by now, you already know who the Katechon is.

It's you.

You are the Katechon which holds back the Apocalypse, you in your obedience to what they demand.

You are the Katechon that restrains you from acting, that sways you away from your will.

You are the Katechon who tells you that you shall die if you act. You will die without Capitalism, without Liberal Democracy, without supermarkets and smartphones, surveillance cameras and taxes, without your strong daddy-leaders, without cops and priests and credit cards, without banks and congress and flags, without your job, without your mortgage, without nuclear weapons and satellites. Without men with guns telling people what to do, you'll die.

You have internalized the will of the powerful, and you think it is your own.

You are the Katechon who tells you what you'll become without them: a Whore, nothing else, male or female or in-between, just a sniveling nothing without them. Without this political order, without these leaders, without the rich, you'll have no way to survive except your body. You'll be an outcast, banished with all the other whores and your mother, Mystery.

# Witches In A Crumbling Empire

You are the Katechon, but maybe you can also hear the serpent saying that you will not die, that there is a world outside the walled gardens of capitalist civilization, that maybe this modern Liberal Democratic order is not worth protecting any longer.

Of course, if you listen to that voice, you might become the Whore who opens those gates, who drowns the cities, and who floods the world.

I say be that Whore.

# *What They Don't Tell You About Vulnerability*

What they don't tell you about vulnerability is that it can end in very cold walks across an iron bridge back to a friend's tiny apartment, a shattered soul cowering under covers.

On a floor I once sat, staring at organic tortilla chips and soy hummus as men talked about being vulnerable. Heart circle, it was called, but I thought I was asked there for a fuck. That night was about vulnerability, cherry tomatoes and something with quinoa, awkward floor cushions, and a tiny bell rung after everyone had been deemed vulnerable enough.

Men baring their hearts, being vulnerable in between the crunch of tortilla chip and slurp of açai berry spritzers, moist warmth like what happens when corpses decompose in hot cars. So much vulnerability I felt a bit fluish, while outside the wet chill beckoned, a last bus or a very cold walk more appealing than listening to other men's performed vulnerability.

Vulnerability is when you were invited to a man's bed but find yourself instead first having to endure a heart circle and you really don't want to be there anymore, but don't have a ride home. And anyway you don't actually have a home, just the promise of one later, one in another country where you don't speak the language and anyway you just wanted something human.

Vulnerability is leaving after the tiny bell is rung one too many times, after too many tortilla chips have been crunched and too much spritzer has been slurped, leaving to catch a bus that doesn't take you where you're staying but it gets you close enough to that iron bridge across which you walk, cold, wet, homeless.

Like the walk cold, wet, homeless after he said you were done, after a year of holding him together, a year after you cowered under a blanket covered in broken glass and drywall, torn clothes and broken computer bits.

Like the walk cold, wet, homeless a year after you cried under covers, cowering though he wasn't there any longer, cowering because he wasn't there any longer but somewhere else, probably in the cold and wet night while you tried to sleep.

Vulnerability is calling your best friend when the door finally slammed and he took off into the night. Vulnerability is brushing off as much of the broken dry wall and glass from your blankets so you could try to sleep though you know you won't, not after that, not while he is out in cold and wet while you shiver alone wondering what you did wrong.

Vulnerability is waking to your best friend stepping over torn books and splintered wood, a shattered chair, broken garden pots and soil, finishing nails and glassless photo frames to reach you. Vulnerability is meeting your best friend's eyes with your own, tears and groans from the glass still in your foot, telling him what happened, admitting you just want him back.

Vulnerability is like the cold wet homeless walk away from your home a year later when all you did to hold him together meant nothing to him, when he told you he was done but you left instead of him because you were better at being homeless than him.

The wet cold walk homeless to a friend's house is the same walk from a heart circle as it is from the end of love, but without the soy hummus and açai berry spritzer.

Vulnerability is being homeless in another country because you were once vulnerable, cowering under blankets as your soul shattered.

Vulnerability is walking across iron bridges in the cold and wet rather than pretend to be vulnerable with people for whom vulnerability means organic tortilla chips and a tiny bell.

Vulnerability is later walking across another bridge in another country, crying over the railings because you have just walked away from the man you love for a little while. Not because it went wrong but because it is going so fucking right.

Vulnerability was walking over that second bridge the first time with him, uncertain what would come but knowing it would change regardless.

Vulnerability is telling him you're scared, not because he is less than what you want or need but because you thought it was only going to be a fuck and now it's become more, more than what you thought you wanted and more than what you thought you needed.

Vulnerability is the moment you tell him you are scared that you don't know how to do this, the moment just before he kissed you and laughed and said you're already doing it. It was in the moment you asked him if there was a formal application process to become his boyfriend, because you were already hooked and it was terrifying you but you wanted to keep doing it anyway.

And then vulnerability was the week after, reading too much from the brevity of his texts, ready to unwrite yourself from this story before it began. It was feeling that raw place, dark like innocence, and not running away.

Vulnerability's the moment you realise your body feels better next to his and not ending it right there. It's rubbing your chest as you leave each time, your hand telling your heart that the ache it feels when you part isn't pain or fear but love.

Vulnerability is deciding to learn that difference.

Vulnerability is admitting you're going to cry when you walk that last time over the bridge, despite the plane ticket you've already bought to see him soon after, despite his own assurances that he is more happy for you than sad.

Vulnerability is how you hear his words and hear behind them how he is trying not to cry, too.

Vulnerability is the moment you hug him good-bye and soak his shirt with your tears, and it's the moment his hand lifts your head to his and see he's crying, too. And it's also the laughter in the moment, laughter with those tears, and the "I love you" and "see you soon," knowing soon will come only as fast as it can, no sooner.

What they don't tell you about vulnerability is that it can end in very cold walks across an iron bridge back to a friend's tiny apartment, a shattered soul cowering under covers.

And that it later can end in walks across a different bridge thousands of miles away, the wind from river to sea drying your tears with laughter.

# The Trade

In a tavern in a port on the shores of an ancient land, I stole from a man his beauty.

He begged it of me, his haggard face beautiful despite his sorrow, his slumped shoulders too well-formed to betray his anguish.

*"Look there in his eyes,"* I heard the crone say.

*"He is in pain, and none will know.*

*"He is alone, and none will approach, assuming always he is with another.*

*"He thinks and feels deeply, but none will hear for the fierce beauty of his eyes dancing to rhythms which are not his.*

*"You can be burdened with too much beauty."*

I stared at him, this man, and stole from him his beauty. Not too much, just enough to make me rue what I had done. His presence no longer commanded distance but coaxed pity, his tired form now naked to the world. I finished my drink, stood from my table, and began to leave. But I could not take my eyes from him, this pitiable man, stripped bare of what made the world forget he could hurt.

Our eyes locked. He smiled, sadly, and I nodded my head.

*"You will give him something in return,"* the crone said, and I suddenly understood her trick.

"I could give his beauty back," I said, but that would be more cruel than theft. I could give him intelligence, I thought, but then knew he already had enough. I could give him wisdom, I started, but then knew I had not enough for myself.

*"What you have in excess he will now need."*

I became angry.

*"What you will give him, you have too much already."*

I grew tired.

*"What will carry him without beauty is what has carried you already too far, over mountains you did not need to climb, through pain you did not need to endure.*

*"What will help him survive the terror of love is what has made you endure too long the sorrow of its absence and the hatred no man should accept.*

*"What will teach him to be more than what he appears has kept you from accepting what you are, striving too long to become more when you have always been enough."*

I began to cry.

"It's all I have," I said to her.

*"Not anymore,"* she replied, turning her face towards mine.

At the door of the tavern I turned to look at the man one last time, and whispered:

"For your beauty which I have stolen, may you endure all things. But not all, only when it serves you.

"For the beauty which you no longer need, may your patience be endless. But not always, only when the person loves you.

"For the beauty which has held you back, may you know how to hold back. But only sometimes, and never out of fear.

"For the beauty which I now hold, may you know you will always survive. But demand more, as I have always failed to do."

I turned to the crone and she smiled, her cracked, weathered skin suddenly beautiful in the grey light outside the tavern. Her beauty was the beauty of the wise: who endure not everything, but only what can be made beautiful.

# *Paganism*™

*We are pitted against an industrial industry which fabricates our dreams for us and insinuates them through our culture and our language. How can we dream when our vocabulary of symbols has only the nuance of newspeak? These are spectres of desire and though marked for sale, remain unattainable.*

*–Peter Grey, Apocalyptic Witchcraft*

*But what if God himself can be simulated, that is to say can be reduced to signs that constitute faith? Then the whole system becomes weightless, it is no longer anything but a gigantic simulacrum – not unreal, but simulacrum, that is to say never exchanged for the real, but exchanged for itself, in an uninterrupted circuit without reference or circumference.*

*–Jean Baudrillard, Simulation and Simulacra*

## Circles For The Stone

Fast past villages with both English and Welsh names he drove us. She sat between us. I tried on her hat. It amused me. It amused them.

And then we were there, the top of an ancient high hill still wet from recent rains. We walked, speaking. I missed some of the threads of our conversation, distracted by the distant vistas. Eyes constantly drawn north:

Gwynedd, Snowdonia, over which dark clouds gathered. The wind echoed a promise reminded, an oath I gave in one of those valleys.

In the remnants of a cromlech we stood, its stones worn down to near nothing by wind and rain. From the centre to the tallest a line formed, extended towards those mountains. It felt important, that stone, that direction, a prehistoric compass directing the eyes to a place wherein something older than stones breathed and waited.

By the "offerings" arrayed at its base, others had thought the stone important, too. Baubles, pink plastic fairies, bracelets, a few slivers of quartz, the coins of empire.

"Neopagan trash," my guide said, sweeping the offerings up in his hands. His eyes burned with something deeper than disgust, and something older. He flung them from the circle with a deft, calm rage. My eyes followed their flight through the air, then met his, then quickly turned away.

"They leave this shit everywhere," he said.

Something about the innocence, or really the pinkness, of the proffered plastic fairy moved me. I imagined some child leaving it, or one of those addled-but-loveable Goddess-type women who are always telling you "we are all-one." Misguided and naïve, but their gesture of offering felt at least benign, harmless.

I said so. I think I said, "There's hope in their search for something authentic. They just don't know what to do yet."

My companions did not answer. They did not need to. As the words spilled out of me, the unbidden image of low-wage Chinese women stamping pink plastic into the form of cartoon-style fairies answered my objection.

## Do We Dare?

*People lose the ability to distinguish between reality and fantasy. They also begin to engage with the fantasy without realizing what it really is. They seek happiness and fulfilment through the simulacra of reality… and avoid the contact/interaction with the real world.*

*--Jean Baudrillard*

A little more than five years ago I stood in an open field, staring into an abyssal sea of stars circling about me, speaking aloud the answer to a question.

Do you dare?

"Yes," I said, losing the ground below me. "I dare."

I cried. My mind shattered. I slept, I didn't sleep. The smell of earth choked me, the stars above my tent screamed distant songs, wheeling as I tried to cling to the wheeling planet upon which I supposedly belonged.

I say five years ago; it might have been forty, the length of my life thus far. I stopped being able to count after that; calendars make no sense any longer, the procession of hours no longer relevant. Only season after season repeating means anything, but even then I cannot clutch to their movement like I once could. Time itself changed, or my place within it. I changed: broken, reforged, broken again, remade, remade, remade.

Before all this I was a chef and a social worker, a partner to a man, a citizen of a city, a denizen of a home. Before all this, Pagan was an identity, like gay or gamer. Paganism was something I liked, a shared interest, an aesthetic. After this, it became the only way I knew how to describe why I slept among stones, sat long nights on fallen trees in cold wet forests. Why I stood shirtless in winter upon a rock as dragon fire shone through a drop of rain falling from a branch, knelt in circles of crow feathers, bled upon an ashen blade, knocked on shields, lay down across rivers, pulled the beards of giants and fucked in moon-silver shadow of antler and branch.

Paganism is the word I've used to explain why I have sat at council with dead hooded men around fires, flew past a guardian into the blood of an enemy and there clotted those hidden streams, turned great edged wheels to grind down the mind of a dangerous fool, stood upon hills watching how some worlds end, why I stole glimpses of toads impaled on pencils and turned that sorcerer's malice into his catastrophic downfall. It is the shorthand for why I have awakened a forest and watched smiling as strangers brought in their gods, ran barefoot through nettles alongside a river of blood, been summoned by children to a tomb across an ocean, argued with the angry hearts of mountains, learned to walk invisible through city streets, and spoken the names that plants call themselves.

But for all the wisdom I've since gathered from bodied and unfleshed teachers guiding me through thick bramble or dark forest, I still didn't know why I called any of this Pagan.

## Paganism, ™

Every word is an utterance for the inexpressible, but once uttered can become the thing itself. To name yourself happy is to leave the moment happiness is meant to describe. Every mystic knows: the moment words are found for the vision, the vision is over.

The land and stars which initiated me into the Other scream of a thing for which Paganism is mere translation. Like all sounds given to the pre-literate, pre-vocal thing-ness below what we call things, its expression can ossify in our mind, wall us from its world. So to name what I have lived and seen and been these last five years "Pagan" has been in some way to betray it.

Yet words waken. A call to arms, a shouted warning to watch out; "I love you" whispered in the trembling of night, "I'm sorry: she's dead" from the lips of a doctor, "fuck you" and "help me": these open gates to new existences even as they close others.

Were it only up to the poets and mystics, the word Pagan would always evoke, always call us outward. Were it only up to me, Pagan would be the sound I make to initiate desire into others, a beckoning into realms of vision and connection.

But it is never up to the poet or the mystic.

Like land that has become property, work that has become labor, and art that has become commodity, Paganism has been enclosed. Paganism is now mostly product, sign without signification, representation without represented. You can go to Pagan conferences, listen to Pagan music, buy Pagan products made by Pagan artisans in Pagan shops. You can read Pagan blogs written by Pagan writers published by Pagan publishers. You can apply Pagan like a label upon any thing you do or say or think, investing by every action and transaction into a Global Brand through which the "Pagan" capitalists draw dividends.

By calling all that I have seen and learned, all that I have written and created, and all that I have known as truth "Pagan," I have inadvertently fed into this branding, improved its market reputation, and helped increase the profits of those for whom Paganism is a thing that can be sold, not a thing to become.

Yet under all this are still my experiences which cannot be sold, the moments of the Other inexpressible, for which I have no other word except Pagan.

The Pagan of the hotel dress-up convention or the pink plastic fairies littering ancient stone exists. We can point to such things, such brandings and say: "here! Here is a Pagan thing." We cannot do the same for the trees at which I stared as I first began to type this, trees beyond which lie the last remnants of the great Celyddon once covering much of Yns Prydein. That cannot be bought. That cannot be branded.

The Witchcraft of the glossy books or online-teachers can be regarded with certainty: this here is "witchcraft." Not true, however, for the moments which I know as witchcraft. A few days ago on the Isle of Skye, encountering my accidental initiator "by chance" upon a street corner just after thinking his name, both of us six thousand miles from where we last lived—that is the Witchcraft I know.

But it is not a thing I can show to you, nor is it a thing I can sell.

A refrain of a song never before sung yet we already, somehow, know the words. An echo from a past we have not yet lived, dreams which speak truth by measures for which we will never find metric. The reflection of sky in water which displays an additional dimension of perception in which we cannot move except in dream: all these things I call Pagan, all these things are my witchcraft. These things cannot be bought.

Witchcraft and Magic and Paganism exist. But they cannot be found through the very means by which we lost them.

## The Greatest Show On Earth

Perhaps because they refuse to shake off their Protestant culture, American Pagans are fond of speaking of the "big tent," under which all the many of "us" gather: Heathens, Polytheists, Occultists, Wiccans, Reclaiming witches and Feri witches, Unitarian-Universalists and solitary practitioners, all crowded under a massive canvas painted blue with white stars like some hokey wizard's hat or, closer to the truth, a U.S. flag without the red- and white- stripes.

The "big tent" is supposed to be about inclusion or some rot, but since it's the same phrase the Democratic Party has used to justify why anti-capitalists, environmentalists, and pro-corporate war-mongers should all be in the same political gathering, there's likely something else happening here. Perhaps what they've always meant isn't "tent" at all, but corral, wall, or internment camp.

Because ultimately, the "big tent" benefits only the vendors of pink plastic fairies, the sleek white gaywitches with their laughable invocations to "The Dark Goddess," the dottering old racist uncles hailing the folk in Alt-Right rallies, the altars photographed and filtered in devotion to the #instawitch hashtag. It does not benefit you, but instead the right-wing Christian corporation that runs a Pagan blog site, the "community news" organization constantly skewing capitalist, nationalist, and ever-so-libertarian, and all the pay-to-pray traditions eager for your money and attention.

The "big tent" isn't a shelter, it's a Market. Within the tent, Paganism isn't a belief or a culture but an interest, spirituality just another thing for you to buy in a world that already has too much shit anyway.

But the story of how Paganism became a product is not just the story of opportunistic women and men seeking profit. It is the story of disenchantment itself. It is the story of displacement and colonization, the wakened horror from which spawned Empire and Nation, Race and Identity. More than anything it is the story of our divorce from land and ourselves, a sickness for which Paganism is sold not as cure but placebo for a necrotic wound we really ought to get checked out.

People seek Paganism to find magic or gods or authentic ways of being and meaning. But the magic and gods have never been gone: they are only buried deep below the asphalt over which they drive, the concrete upon which they walk, the steel and cement in which they live. The gods of rivers are buried beneath the cities, poisoned; we wipe our asses with the corpses of forest gods. The magic of human will and sense is psychologized, medicalized: "aberrant" perceptions of the myriad are disciplined or drugged out of us, then sold back to us on spiritual retreats.

The search for authentic meaning and ways of being which draws people to Paganism springs from a rejection of what else is on offer, a malaise of what is available to us by the Modern: 40-hour work weeks, concrete housing blocks, relentlessly mediated life in which too many of us only see breath-taking views of forests or communal celebrations on screens. Those depictions—pixelated, fed and filtered through Instagram feeds or used as mere backdrop for mythic television series like Vikings or Game Of Thrones—serve not to draw us closer to what we seek, but push us even more distant from the world we have lost.

## Magic Is Everything But What You Can Buy

*And so art is everywhere, since artifice is at the very heart of reality. And so art is dead, not only because its critical transcendence is gone, but because reality itself, entirely impregnated by an aesthetic which is inseparable from its own structure, has been confused with its own image. Reality no longer has the time to take on the appearance of reality. It no longer even surpasses fiction: it captures every dream even before it takes on the appearance of a dream.*

Jean Baudrillard

# Witches In A Crumbling Empire

We search for the authentic in the only place it cannot be found. We seek the gods and spirits not in the land around us but in empty symbols, poorly-written books and "mystery traditions" led by leaders for whom their unwitting initiates are their only way of getting laid.

We scroll endlessly through blogs promising to teach us how do magic, purchase special oils and candles to stave off the terror of modern life and maybe make us not feel so lonely. When none of that works, we try again, and again, forgetting that magic has nothing to do with what you buy or which online-tradition gave you a certificate of completion.

Magic has nothing to do with the teachers of magic, the vending tables at the "cons" or the Etsy shop, none of which are much different from the pink plastic fairy left at the base of a stone.

Magic is you.

It has always been you, you and the world around you. Magic is the breathing forests, the scream of owl and raven as you wander alone through darkness. Magic is in the stars above and the stars you see after your eyes close, the wind from distant mountains and the loamy breath of the grave.

Magic is the stone, and it is also the circle, and especially in all the forgotten wisdom with which ancients living millennia before anyone called themselves "Pagan" raised theose stones.

Magic is what it has always meant to be human, before the makers of the pink plastic fairies and the ringmasters of the Big Tent set up shop.

Magic, connection to the earth, the experience of the Other—these things the merchants of Paganism™ cannot sell us, and the fact that they try is proof they have never experienced those things themselves.

Let them be honest. They all only selling books and candles, art and skills. Let these things be judged on those qualities, without the false promises and dishonest marketing.

And let us all be honest: the real magic is the world the Capitalists have been selling off from under our feet, the real connection is our reclamation of the earth, and the real Paganism is resistance to the commodification of all that it means to be human.

# *It All Tastes Of Sorrow*

A dark line of trees; past them, a darker line of mountains, gray-blue clouds obscuring the last light of day. Though it does not get dark this far north at summer solstice, even the most direct of sun illuminates with a sorrow indescribable.

We sat staring at that dark line of trees and past them the darker line of mountains.

"It all tastes of sorrow," I told him.

"It will for weeks," he replied. "Each time."

It all tastes of sorrow: mountains ringing the soul with brutal indifference, the way giants stride across the earth or a human crushes grass underfoot. It all tastes of sorrow: the water dripping from peat into streams which crash over rock into loch and then sea. It all tastes of sorrow: rook and raven wheeling over glens cleared out to make way for the new order of Capital.

Some vistas make you gasp for air, others make you sigh: choking inhale, long exhale—these are the breaths of shuddering grief, sobbing alone as you clutch the pillow upon which they'll never sleep again. It is not joy with which you greet each new sight, but its more sombre, serious twin.

# Witches In A Crumbling Empire

I had no expectations for my visit to Scotland. Like others my age, I watched Braveheart as a teenager, found myself both moved by the film's sweeping scenes and tormented by Mel Gibson's over-dramatic acting, shrinking into my seat in terror when the theatre audience laughed and applauded when the male consort of the English prince was pushed to his death from a tower. Enticing as they are supposed to be, none of the aesthetic reproductions of Scotland nor its packaged cultural products (Scotch, formal bagpipes) ever fascinated me.

Of the Celtic lands, only Bretagne and Wales seduce me. But I have had to leave the former for three months on account of border laws which seem more distant from how the world ought to work than they did when I marched in solidarity with refugees in America.

Perhaps it is because I, too, am now a refugee, currently stateless as I will never return to the United States. On account of laws I unfortunately am too cowardly to disobey, I left Bretagne for Scotland. My best friend offered a road-trip to the Highlands, his sacred land, and thus I am here, sharing visions of beauty and sorrow. Later we will be in Wales, and then I will be in Dublin, waiting out my enforced exile until it ends on the Equinox.

Perhaps this is my sorrow, the grief with which I greet this land. An exile wandering places to which he does not belong, climbing mountains which do not know him, standing in groves of birch and alder along river banks listening to yet another language into which I was not born. Perhaps it is this, and also more: none of the trails along which I've walked lead home, nor to any place I know. Where home is, though, is a land which, though I longed dreamt of being within it, became fully foreign once I entered its gates.

The grief is of those gates, and what dreams I shed to enter them. Loves I will never encounter again, hopes which now mean nothing, possibilities in currency too small to exchange. All that, left as so many old garments bagged and tossed into charity bins, with a wistful sigh and then a panicked questioning whether I'd checked all the pockets for change.

The grief is of those gates, and also other gates. Not just the departure gate to Manchester, but the gate into the realms of the dead which I saw again upon a hill before I left Bretagne. Not just those gates, but also the doors into powerful magic I cannot comprehend swinging open unbidden. Not just those gates, but the one into myself, through which lingers the deepest of sorrows.

Perhaps this is all just Scotland and its dead speaking. It passes that way more than I will ever understand; Peter Grey said the witch is created by the land to speak for it, and perhaps this is also what he meant. We do not so much speak for the land as translate for it.

To translate the sorrow of the land you must both become the land and its sorrow. And so it is for these reasons the dark line of trees above the dark line of mountains tastes of sorrow.

It is the land's sorrow, it is my sorrow, and we taste it together on each others' lips.

# *Gift of Crow, Gift of Stag*

The floor of my room was covered in crow feathers. At least three hundred of them, originally laid out in a spiraling pattern around a center which was me. But then I started drinking, and the pattern changed, scattered, each disassociating from the other along with my thoughts.

A lover moved out five weeks before. It was better this way: when he'd told me he was leaving I felt only relief, a great crushing weight upon my chest no longer crushing. I tried to act like I was bothered—that's what you do, yes, when someone is one thing and then another and you are hoping they will decide and they finally do?

Never mind him. The next lover was the reason I was sitting in a spiral of feathers, drinking. I was maybe also crying, because that is what you do when all you have is feathers and some beer and confusion.

I'd met the cause of all those feathers five weeks before, the day the lover decided to move out.

I made the mistake of showing him some of those feathers, not all of them, because I didn't have all them yet. I showed him right after such intensity that he looked terrified of what we were about to become. I was terrified too, but told him anyway, "I think I'm falling in love with you."

His answer was silence, a full two years of it, but anyway who cares when you see him again in a grocery line and he's scared shitless, hoping you don't notice he's right in front of you.

The feathers didn't scare him, I know now. It was the "I think I'm falling..." part, the part you're never supposed to tell another man ever, the part I tell much more often than never. But I decided it was the feathers, and all that came with it. Witch-shit, dirt from graves and dead voices, the stuff that had become my life. Who wants a man who's into that stuff around? Even worse when that man also was starting to fall in love and didn't care that he wasn't supposed to say it.

I know the feathers probably didn't scare him, and anyway, I'd only had a quarter as many before he ghosted me. I found the rest the day he did, in a park not far from where I lived. Late summer is when the crows moult. They rook together in that park, hundreds of them, leaving feathers everywhere even when not moulting. But that day, the day he'd become a ghost, they were everywhere, the fields black with them, and I had a backpack and pockets and some sorrow and also a cell phone.

"This always happens," I texted a friend on that phone.

"What's happening?" he asked.

"I'm gathering crow feathers in a park crying. I think I just got ghosted again."

I returned that night with over two hundred crow feathers. I counted them, laid them out in a spiral and drank and then passed out, waking to a room that looked like murder.

This piece isn't about him, though. Nor the guy before. It's about me, and also the guy who came after. It's about the coward I became after all that, with only feathers and ghosts to keep me company. And about the guy who kept company with ghosts and feathers who proved to me I wasn't a coward at all.

We met on one of those apps on a phone. He woofed me or something, I woofed him back. He sent a message: "Nice photos. I like your arms a lot. I'll be in your city in three months for a show—let's have a beer."

Men don't normally make dates three months in advance. Men also don't play music for dying people or make art from dead birds.

He did.

I found myself staring at his pictures. One of them was a piece of his art, a fucking dead crow. That would have been enough, were he not also brutally fucking hot.

# Witches In A Crumbling Empire

We exchanged a few more messages. I was already planning to be in his city two weeks from then, and could I buy him a beer?

"Damn," he replied. "I go on tour the day before."

We'd have a beer three months thence, it seemed. Which seemed absurd. More absurd then all the crow feathers I had in my bedroom. More absurd then the dead-bird art he made. Not as absurd as what I did then.

He had a show in a week. I had time. I changed my plans, and didn't tell him, and just showed up.

Maybe other people do that, I don't know. I don't, and definitely not after three months of pretty wretched self-loathing, the sort you wallow in after several men in succession all turn down your advances without reason, one of them ghosts you after five intense weeks together, and not much else in your life seems to be going right for you to just brush it all off.

That stuff makes you a coward after awhile. You stop believing in yourself, stop trying, and tell yourself you're better off alone. But of course, you don't actually feel better off, and you know you're lying to yourself, which then makes you feel like a traitor to the one guy who seems to keep sticking around, sleeping in your bed every night since you were born.

I decided I wouldn't be a coward. I think it was the dead birds, actually. We had that much in common, anyway.

I went down the next week, stayed with a friend, and then went to his show the next day.

The bar where his band played was small, painted all black, one of those awkward places where you don't really have a place to sit and standing seems wrong. I drank, maybe too much, waiting for his set to start.

He'd sent me links to his music. The stuff's gorgeous, haunting as fuck, music evoking death and vengeance and wet misted forests where all the branches cast shadows from distant moonlight so that you're not certain if you are surrounded by trees or antlers.

When I first heard it, all the crow feathers scattered across my room made sense again, as did everything else in my world.

They began. I found a place to sit, not so close that I'd look like I was stalking. Maybe I was; maybe he didn't mind. They began, and I no longer cared whether it was strange I'd changed my plans to see his show and ask him out on a date after. I no longer cared that I'd ever cried in my life, no longer cared that anyone thought me odd or strange. They began, and all the ghosts I'd ever known, the dead ones and the living who'd fled, suddenly seemed my family, like I was a ghost too, a ghost to myself.

I forgot what I'd meant to do while they played. I almost didn't re-member afterwards, as the crowd milled back to the bar and he stood be-hind a table, selling CD's and shirts. I almost left, then changed my mind, walked up to him, started to say hello.

He gave me a hug. "Hey—you came! How long are you here for?"

I fumbled with something in my pocket. "Yeah. Uh, I'll be here 'till Sunday." I found what I was looking for. It was ridiculous. But seemed right. "You were awesome."

"Thanks. We had some sound trouble. Want to get a beer tomorrow?"

I nodded. I hadn't known how to ask. He asked instead. I felt really okay with this.

"This is for you." I poured some dirt in his hand. "It's from Karl Marx's grave."

"Oh, awesome!" He answered. This wasn't going poorly.

The next day, I took a bus to the same bar to meet him again. Except it wasn't the right bus, and I ended up far from the city and really confused. I texted him, he thought it was funny, he didn't mind waiting for me. An hour and a half after I was supposed to arrive I finally got there, and texted him to tell him so.

He showed up twenty minutes later. While I waited, I wrote in my journal about the absurd thing I'd just done. I'd never traveled to another city to see someone I wanted to meet without any guarantee he'd actually want to meet me back. I never chanced anything, not like this, not with someone so beautiful or brilliant or bizarre.

I wrote, "you brave fucker–you just changed your life."

We drank, talked. I don't remember what we talked about, only that we seemed to understand the other enough that when there was silence, it was the comfortable sort. At some point he leaned into me, I held him, ran my hand along the back of his neck. He felt good. I seemed to feel good to him. You don't always know unless someone tells you, but with him I knew.

"I need to catch a bus back," I said. I was drunk, it was pouring rain, the last bus was in a few minutes.

"I haven't been with a guy in three months," he said. "But if you don't mind that, than I'm taking you home with me."

We go to his place. We have to pass through a basement practice space to get to his room. I'm drunk and need some water, he's drunk and does too, and I don't really know how he got my clothes off so fast between the glass of water and the part that still almost shuts me down in pure wonder.

# Witches In A Crumbling Empire

Everyone's got the parts of their body they don't like, the bits they wish looked different. You can see these in the way people dress, where they wear extra clothes, what cuts of fabric they choose. Study series of photographs of a person and these shadow-places become even more obvious, the selfies taken of the same side of the face each time, the lighting chosen, the way they stand in mirrors. In person, you can scent them out by their posture, what side they always keep turned or what parts of the body they always tense around people they find attractive or people they want to impress, the parts which relax when they no longer need to be guarded.

"I like this," he said, licking the very part of my chest I was hoping he would ignore. "And this," he said, rubbing his face against the part of my stomach I wished was invisible to the world.

He found every one of those places first before the parts I'd hoped he see instead, assaulting every lack of self-confidence with a witch-lust that within seconds had my cock leaking so much precum I was soaked.

He found that too, stared at my cock. What men know, that women often do not, is that men are unwillingly reduced to our cocks. It is the only part of our bodies we are allowed to be sexual with, both with others and with ourselves. Men send dick-picks because they're reduced to their phallus, what they can produce for others, not who they are. It's twice-worse for gay men than for straights, who at least are excused their emotional idiocy because that is what is expected of them.

The cock is the final reveal. It's what makes or breaks everything for another, or what we're told is supposed to. Too small, too big, not ugly, too cut, too uncut—it all too often comes down to that. Why not cut to the chase, if that's all you're really wanted for in the first place?

"Dude, awesome." He said, running his tongue along it.

When you find a guy like that, you don't sleep. You might have been tired, but you aren't anymore. You doze, sure; then he wakes you by gnawing on your nipples or throating your cock and you're fully awake again, flipping him over, pinning him, following the lines of all his tattoos with your tongue while he writhes under you, rubbing your beard against his ass and neck and face before dozing again and starting over.

The same sort of guy who lusts after all the parts you try hide are also the sort of guys who wake other stuff in you, drives and desires and strength you hide from others. You hide the fact you want to drive this sort of guy hard into a wall, break all the plaster with his head, and he's pulled it out of you before you know it. He's not begging for it, he's forcing it out of the cage you forge for it, prying it out of you because he sees it lurking and wants it free.

You can't be timid after that, can't be a coward, can't hide from yourself or anyone else. Someone who's you is mauling him, and he's mauling you back, and nothing's going back into a cage again ever.

Ten hours later, we're done, maybe two hours of sleep between us. Clothes on, stumbling into grey morning rain, catching a bus, silent. He was awkward. So was I. That wasn't like anything I'd ever done. Maybe it wasn't for him, either.

After his tour, I came down again. We went to the same bar, went back to his place, had the same sort of night. The next morning, I thought about asking him if he'd maybe want to do this more often. With that same skill with which he found and lusted after every part of myself I did not like, saved me the awkwardness of asking.

"I'm moving across the country in a few months. I can't have a boy-friend."

"Friends, then?" I asked, choking sorrow.

"Yeah," he answered.

I saw him one last time.

He was playing another show. I went, sat as close to his feet as I could while chewing on a sprig of rosemary I picked on my way there.

The music felt even better, more otherworldly. Like the dark stories of faeries, or in the Welsh tales of forests, I felt myself getting lost amongst the trees, trying to find my way along paths led only by distant calls of unseen crows.

"I have a gift for you," I said afterward.

The headboard on his bed had a carving of a stag-head on it. When I wasn't looking at his body those nights, I found myself looking at it, its image seared into my dreams afterward almost stronger than his. I handed my gift to him; forty crow feathers stuffed inside a gnawed stag vertebrae I'd found at an ancient Heathen site in Alsace. It felt like an offering to a god, or whomever his god was.

"Awesome," he said, tracing the gnaw marks. "Mice?"

"Squirrels. They gnaw the bones to get calcium in the winter."

He looked happy. He took it, and thanked me.

I thanked him, too.

# Magic Waiting Beyond Running Feet

I have to find a new magic because it is telling me to find it, because I hear the thunder of running feet through streets and the crash of falling stone and broken glass and it waits behind all that, or just before.

It is easy to ignore, isn't it, here where rivers carry away the dreams of sleepers down to the sea which drowned Ys, when the great floodgates broke because she no longer cared to keep their world together, no longer cared for their dreams that kept the world together.

I walk past their world and their dreams, along the rivers. I even ran, the earth surging up from my feet back from the city of metal scraps where they greeted me with warm bearded kisses. Their dreams taste foreign, are beer-drenched, hidden from view by shutters closed by generations before them, generations who heard a previous rumble: unlatched, unfolded, pulled tight, and latched again.

We are here again. I am here again, much bigger, bearing more fragments of selves (that are not me, that are become me) like clothing upon my towering body which cannot find a roof.

We are here again, the towers and their lords overlooking land worked by women and men who do not want them, who sharpen their scythes and talk in ever-less-quiet voices of what they intend to do.

I do not know what I intend to do.

I am here again, we are here again, and when last we were here the watching towers called for war. Dreams behind shuttered windows disturbed, bags packed, kisses from mothers on unbearded faces, *"au revoirs"* when what was needed were *"adieus."* Elsewhere, other towers, other doors, other kisses, other partings to graves made of open fields where raven and crow picked clean their bones like Brân's.

Where are their heads now? Where is his head now? Where will mine finally lie?

I met the Wanderer before ravens danced on the hill where I sat outside Oslo. A fucking glass eye like I needed the joke, I'm eating ice cream on a bench, and he asked me what I desire.

I desire to be here, I said, and he said he'd like to go to America, maybe be on a screen.

The Wanderer is here again, and we are for awhile each other. Brân fucked me by a lake, but he'll fuck me on that tree, our eye sockets still dripping blood, looking before and after at what the dreams of others means.

Sometimes when I walk the crows hide me, but I remember watching Brâns bones picked clean, white like chalk. There's a fucking crow staring at me now as I write, like some joke we're all sharing about the man about to lose his head and finally become his own.

His own in the breaking glass, the falling stone, the terrified crowds seeking shelter from the towers who've prescribed this slaughter, calculated, budgeted the cost of lost intractable workers.

I do not know what I intend to do, except find that magic waiting for me past the running feet over cobble, beyond the slamming shutters, over the breaking glass.

# Bastard Children of a Slaughtering Empire

I woke into world the bastard child of a slaughtering Empire. I woke into world in an old Shawnee town, but I am not Shawnee, and the town is their ghost.

The town, in Shawnee, is called Chalawgatha, which is also the name of the band of Shawnee who lived there. Wherever they settled, they settled in Chalawgatha, because they were the Chalawgatha, and so Chalawgatha was their town.

What is the ghost of their town is a sprawl of mid-western pavement called Chillicothe, Ohio. Chillicothe sits alongside a dirtied river on the last plainslands before the land roils upward into the ancient soft-green Appalachian mountains. Chalawgatha was a small settlement upon that same river with much smaller, hand-built mounts rising from the earth. Once the Algonquin ancestors of the Shawnee traveled those time-worn mountains and buried their dead beneath raised hills. The hearts of those mountains are coal; the hearts of those mounds are bone.

It's doubtful the Chalagawtha Shawnee suspected that one day both mount and mound would be laid low.

## Homes of Hillfolk Upon Open Graves

Where I woke into the world is a beautiful, haunted place, forested hills whispering ancient truths from caves and streams, wildflower-strewn vales singing fairy-tale beauty into the souls of mortals. It is also a land trashed, paved-over, blown up to get the coal from the heart of the great mountain-spirits, razed to plunder the trees clinging to their face like verdant beards.

Where I woke into this world is sometimes filmed for European documentaries on American poverty, images of shoeless dirt-faced children montaged alongside shoeless dark-skinned children in Los Angeles.

I had shoes; my neighbors did not. Water poured from our tap, my neighbors drew from an arsenic-tainted well. Our sewer overflowed and opened, feeding tree-tall grasses and milkweeds; my neighbours shat in a shed.

We were poor. Others were more poor. The race to the bottom is an abyss mirroring the race to the top, smog-filled skies reflected in sludge filled pools. The wealthiest can always have more wealth, the poorest can always have less.

Unlike others in those European documentaries, I was never filmed. I did not know my poverty except that I was told of it on television and from my violent and abusive father, who threw crumpled beer cans against a black and white television as Ronald Reagan told us how the Union fared. Then there were the commercials for colas, and shoes, and things we could never afford but others must could, because why would the television tell people to buy things for which they had no money?

When it rained, our clay yard turned slippery, light-brown slicks pooling water into drainage ditches along the rural highway gouged through those winding hills. It was sloppy, and clay is a relentless sort of mud, but I would play for hours. I liked the world best during those rains and just after, the air finally cleansed for a few hours from the moldy garbage-smell of the paper mill along the Scioto river and the rotten sewage smell from our overfilled sewer.

The Chalagawtha Shawnee likely did not worry much over the smell of the paper mill. Nor did they wait like I did for the food trucks from the government, laden with brown paper-board boxes filled with processed cheese, dried milk-powder, and enriched rice. They did not clear space in their clay yards for each autumn's delivery of blue-black coal for their wood-burning stoves. They did not pass by vales and hollows filled with rusting enameled machine-parts and used plastic diapers. They did not wonder at the strange pains and stranger thoughts entering their head from the nuclear plant just to the south.

We moderns, particularly the Pagan sort, are accused of romanticizing the past. I try not to make that mistake, but it's difficult to imagine the slaughtered and displaced Chalagawtha Shawnee lived lives as miserable, as nasty, as brutish and as short as we're taught to believe. At least not until Empire came.

## "Indians" like gods

I woke into the world as an American, not as a Shawnee, a child of Empire and Capital, descended from displaced peasants from many other lands. From my father ran blood of Alsatians, Swabians, French, Irish and Welsh; from my mother came more French and Welsh and a bit of English.

I was formed from the blood and semen of peoples without title, wealth or trades. Displaced and impoverished people crafted the homunculus of me, mewling in an aluminum trailer. I was born the bastard heir of Colonialism, suckling not at the teat of imperial wealth pumps but upon rags dipped in the vats of government charity.

I knew none of this then. Empire was a thing elsewhere, wealth the currency of cities on the other side of those low mountains.

Slaughter of peoples, when you are a child, is for the story-books and the 3 channel-reception of the small glowing screen: cowboys shooting Indians, Romans burning Heathens and Christians, Hitler marching Jews to ovens. Ancient peoples and their gods were all over-ocean and under farflung skies, not by the low mound by which I played and napped.

Ancestors from over an ocean settled in untouched forests, unwitting footsoldiers of Imperial reach, pushing the descendents of mound-builders ever westward, as if chased by an unseen, voracious monster from which all peoples knew to flee. Wars fought between the settlers' government and the tribal confederacies always ended poorly for the defenders, but what became of these lands cannot be described as glorious or even civil.

The Chalagawtha Shawnee settled in towns nearby the burial mounds of their Algonquin ancestors. They were built during periods named in the American fashion, the Hopewell and Adena cultures, after the names of the settlers' estates where their mounds were identified. The Chalagawtha town along the Scioto river was near a collection of mounds named now, in even more American fashion, "Mound City."

From that Chalagawtha near Mound City by the Scioto river came the most famous Shawnee, and the most antagonistic to Empire, Tecumseh. Traveling with his brother, a prophet given to visions of coming storms and calamities, he led a resistance of confederated Creek and Shawnee tribes against that westward push.

Tecumseh was killed in battle in 1831, far from Chalagawtha. But he would return eighty-five years later to those mounds, at least for a few years, by way of an orphaned child of settlers who went on to burn cities to the ground. Seven years after Tecumseh's death, Tecumseh Sherman was born, later christened "William Tecumseh Sherman" by his adoptive mother. His father, a lawyer in Lancaster, Ohio, had developed a fascination for the Shawnee hero, gifting the name to one of his children but dying without giving them anything else. Raised by a wealthy politician instead, William Tecumseh Sherman later became the general who would order "Hard War," the scorched-earth tactic which saw Atlanta and other southern cities become settlements of flames.

General Sherman died in 1891 in New York City and was buried in St. Louis, Missouri, both far from Chalagawtha. But 16 years later, as the United States entered the first global imperial war, the Union he'd helped preserve built a training and supply installation along the Scioto River atop the mostly-flat plainsland. Flat, except for a few small man-made hills.

Mound City was razed to make way for global war, the birthplace of General Sherman's namesake buried under a military fort. There, in old Chalagawtha, men trained to join an imperial power in fighting other imperial powers in trenches gouged into the land from whence the settlers who'd displaced the Shawnee came. It's totemic, and also a really bad joke.

## "Their graves turned into ploughed fields"

The mounds of Chalagawtha were later excavated and rebuilt—Camp Sherman was dismantled in 1920—and the remains catalogued and distributed. Some went overseas, kept as a sampling of colonized cultures in the British Museum in London, others displayed in the visitor center. I went to the visitor center at Mound City, visited that mounded center of Chalagawtha. I remember looking at those relics, a child ten years of age, confused. There was lots of mica, some wood, a little copper, all from an age when "real Indians" lived and fought and died, before the coming of cities and cables.

That year—I do not remember if before or after my visit–I had learned there were still-living Indians, though I could perhaps be forgiven for disbelieving it. Cable had just been lain along the ridge-line where I lived, so I'd now seen so many more stories of the killings of First Nations people that they'd become as mythic as unicorns or gods.

A "real-life Indian" came to my school that year, dressed in white tasseled deerskin leather. I remember asking him—I had to, I'd been fooled before—if he were really an Indian, because they were all dead. He laughed, and smiled, and said "some of us are still alive." But he looked a little sad, and very honest.

I hadn't believed in Indians, the way I hadn't believed in gods. I'd read the stories of their existence, knew they'd once roamed the earth, but surely they'd all gone under the earth like Zeus and Apollo by now. And here was a real-life Indian, one who'd somehow survived the coming of settlers and refrigerators. He was Choctaw, I remember. He made certain we knew this, that he wasn't "from here," but from elsewhere.

The Choctaw were known as one of the "Five Civilized Tribes" on account of their early peace treaties and alliances with the United States. When the Chalagawtha Shawnee chief Tecumseh met with the Choctaw leaders and pleaded their help against the settlers and colonists, he was not only rebuffed but threatened by Pushmatah, the Choctaw leader, who vowed to fight those who fought against the United States. In a transcribed speech to the Choctaw, Tecumseh warned their relationship with the new imperial state would not go well:

> Where today are the Pequot? Where are the Narragansett, the Mochican, the Po-canet, and other powerful tribes of our people? They have vanished before the avarice and oppression of the white man, as snow before the summer sun ... Sleep not longer, O Choctaws and Chickasaws ... Will not the bones of our dead be plowed up, and their graves turned into plowed fields?

Tecumseh was right. Pushmatah, who had organized Choctaw warriors to fight against Tecumseh's Creek alliance, died 11 years after Tecumseh in Washington D.C., there to beg the government for redress against white squatters of Choctaw land. And six years after Pushmatah's death, the Treaty of Dancing Rabbit Creek was signed, granting the U.S. full control over all traditional Choctaw lands, despite their decades of alliance against bellicose natives.

I do not know if the Choctaw man who spoke to our class thought much on this matter, nor did any of us children know enough to ask on that tragedy. I do know now that he was not the first "real-life Indian" I'd met. Adjacent the clay-pit upon which my home stood lived my friends, whose always-tanned skin, even in the heart of winter, was an embarrassment to them but a matter of fascination for me. And off the ridge, in the small ghost township called Knockemstiff, lived several families without running water, whose body odor was an unfortunate source of jeer and amusement to us elementary school children; their kids shoeless except in deepest winter when they walked clumsily in adult boots many inches too big for their feet.

## Angry Lands, Haunted Peoples

It's tempting to see the re-appearance of Tecumseh to the site of his birth in the form of Camp Sherman as mere co-incidence or accidental poetry. But the dead haunt us for a reason, and if we're to have any hope of revolt, we cannot ignore these spectres. Besides, the United States military has an intimate relationship to the slaughtering of First Nations peoples–the same military which Pagans begged to include Pentagrams and Mjolnir on headstones was responsible for the slaughter at Wounded Knee and the countless other slaughters of indigenous folk.

Ward Churchill has shown that the yellow ribbon to "support our troops," those jingoistic magnets on automobiles traversing highways built over the corpses of buffalo, come from the scarves worn by U.S. soldiers during the 'Indian Wars.' Even now, the military names weapons and military vehicles after conquered peoples (as Noam Chomsky mentions, "We might react differently if the Luftwaffe were to call its fighter planes "Jew" and "Gypsy"), and the US military unapologetically code-named Osama Bin Laden, "Geronimo."

The United States is all one vast grave of slaughtered peoples. Our subdivisions, our malls, our kindergartens and Pagan bookshops are all lain over stolen land. And not just stolen, but currently-in-the-process-of-being-stolen. In Seattle I lived on stolen Duwamish land; and they, whose river is a Superfund site poisoned by industry and occupied by a war-machine manufacturer, are not even recognised as a tribe despite their very real existence. In fact, like the homeless, like the sacred, like global warming, like the poisoned earth in places like Appalachia, Capital and Empire merely pretend its own apocalypse, its own slaughter doesn't exist. But so do we.

Our disenchantment is mere denial, springing from our separation from the land and ourselves. It's horrifying to make a connection between the places we live and the rivers of blood and sagas of sorrow which cleared the land for our single-family homes and hipster restaurants, or even our sacred sanctuaries. This is Marx's "estranged labor," expanded by Silvia Federici's work, the way we separate aspects of our being, classify our activities, and Enclose certain experiences from other experiences, living disjointed, fractured existences, alienated from and terrified of interwoven threads of meaning.

Animism can shatter these categories. Paganism's supposed to, but can't if it continues to cling to the benefits of Empire. Animist peoples know this, but we bastard children of Empire, do not. Being disenchanted, utterly disassociated from the land means we can't even trace the threads between the "benefits" of modern civilization and the slaughter of peoples.

## Appalachia is the World

Nowhere is this more evident than Appalachia, the place where both Tecumseh and I were born.

Much of Appalachia comprises what some call "exclusion zones," and they are essential for the existence of Capitalism, as well as most of what makes modern life so(-called) civilized. In exclusion zones, Capitalism functions precisely as it did when it first started, poisoning the water and air, raping the land for resources like coal and wood, and keeping the population in conditions quite similar to early 19th century peasants. There used to be many more such places in the United States, but in the last fifty years, as environmentalism took hold and terror of acid rain, smog-filled cities, cancer, and developmental disabilities finally took hold, Capitalists altered their behavior slightly.

They didn't stop wasting the planet, polluting the air and water, or making miserable the lives of people. Instead, they just moved it elsewhere, hid it from the view of the consumers whose purchases give consent to all this exploitation. They moved accumulation to exclusion zones, benefiting from (and propagating) myths about the backwardness of the people in those areas which helped ensure those who didn't see that damage never took seriously the accounts of people experiencing it.

Thus, in American discourse, Appalachians are stupid hicks, backwards, violent conservatives (or militants), uneducated, and not worth listening to. And if you've followed anything at all about the recent protests over the murders of unarmed Black men in the United States, you're probably seeing a parallel. The same that is said of people in exclusion zones in the United States is said of Black people, and this is not by accident.

The plight of the Appalachian whose water is poisoned by coal mining is similar to the Midwesterner whose water is poisoned by fracking, and both are similar again to the plight of the Black family living in Detroit or Baltimore in abject poverty with their water being turned off. And the similarities don't end there: they all suffer the same lack of resources, lack of education, high crime rates, indifferent and often oppressive government representatives, and a great silencing of their voices constructed through prejudices regarding education, lifestyle, culture, and family structures.

These groups are all similar to those living in exclusion zones around the world, where the overwhelming amount of damage and destruction wrought by Capitalism is displaced. Razed forests, poisoned rivers, dried-up wells, toxic waste, abject poverty, unbreathable air: these are the foul spirits birthed by Capitalist greed, but we don't see it. The same process which keeps us from seeing the Dead, the spirits, the fae, and the gods keeps us from seeing the Chinese labourer attempting to kill herself rather than make another iPad, from seeing the connection between our automobiles and U.S. Imperialism, our electricity and mountain-top removal, our comfortable lives and the constant wars in the Middle East.

It feels like we're waiting for an inheritance we'll never get and we are not owed. Empire's slaughter cleared land for the coming of displaced Europeans like my own family, but it doesn't care about me, only my submission, only my silence. It also doesn't care about you, either, except that you buy what it's got to sell, stare at screens on your way to your jobs, and keep denying the connections between your security and all the people that have to die to make you feel safe.

The dead Black kid in the street is also the slaughtered Lakota at Wounded Knee, and they are both also the drowned Syrian refugee, the shoeless cancer-ridden Appalachian, and all die in the name of Empire. Perhaps we, Empire's bastard children, will finally take their side instead.

# *Change*

Perhaps your shoes and mine will one day look
like the change you thought had fallen from your pocket.
It had fallen from mine, I remember,
when still wearing clothes I
turned in bed to kiss you
and it fell.
You took it as you left and
I watched,
smiling,
saying nothing.
I'm still smiling, because I would have done the same,
not noticing it wasn't mine that had fallen, but yours.
And perhaps you would have watched too and said nothing either,
like later on perhaps we'll say nothing
about our shoes on the floor
unneeded, for awhile at least,
like change fallen from pockets
strewn about like our clothes,
discarded like our fears.

# *That Feeling Again,*
# *Mr. Frog*

There's that feeling again, Mr. Frog. You ever feel it?

Mr. Frog's staring back at me from atop the horizontal support beam for my nephew's swing set. He's got such human gestures, crosses his arms, his long spindly fingers resting serene against the wood. So calm he is, staring back at me with one eye. What's he looking at with the other? Probably the moon. She's big, she's quite bright, looming over the silver-tasseled oaks. All Ceridwen-like.

I'm watching his throat pulse. Is that his heart or his lungs? Fast, fast, small hearts beat fast, our big hearts beat slow. Fast is for those who live fast, and short. Slow is for the ponderous, though we go too fast, Mr. Frog, like we've got somewhere to go.

Mr. Frog's got nowhere to go. He drapes an arm down the side of the beam now, all relaxed-like. The moon looms above us both, like Ceridwen, like the death waiting for us when our hearts, tiny-fast and large-slow, don't got more beats in them.

There's that feeling again, Mr. Frog. You ever feel it? Like when all life's good, so good, so full and safe. Walled garden, the falconer's quiet wisdom surrounded by coins. Sated with all the world, aware there's a world past that low wall. Look over it? Set the falcon flying, screeching like the hawk I heard this morning (I think you might've been asleep, Mr. Frog)? Set the falcon flying, or set out the dinner, either way's so calm, so perfect. Tiny hearts beat fast and end quick, the large ones stumble, seize, and make all kinds of scenes.

I'm about to make a scene, aren't I? That's that feeling there, Mr. Frog. You ever feel it? That moment you're all complete and then you're not, some fragment outside yourself, of yourself, heart tugging outward like gravity what forget its center. Like you forgot your center, except your center ain't always complete because we ain't meant to be alone, Mr. Frog.

You get that feeling sometimes, Mr. Frog? You with one eye on the moon and one eye on me, waiting, catching mosquitoes with your tongue, the ones biting me because of that one deal I made with the Mothers. I still laugh when I think 'bout that, no blood, you don't get blood, besides the whole world's got my blood.

Mr. Frog, you got my blood now. You're welcome.

Mr. Frog, you get that feeling when the whole world makes screaming sense, wheeling like that hawk each morning when I take my tea, 'cept it's been smoothies lately and a half-hour on the wheel? Moving iron 'round with arms meant for holding someone, arms hoisting my nephews in the air to my shoulders, arms resting on my side while my fingers clack-clack to make pixels appear, arms much busier than yours, Mr. Frog.

The world gets to wheeling like she does, you're all complete and done and here we are suddenly ascending. Like the gravity what forgot its center, your slow lumbering heart pulled towards something you don't know what. Mostly the earth pulls you and you're all good, doing your work, sipping whey and hemp and coco nibs and strawberries before doing your clack-clack on the keys and moving bits of iron around.

And then the moon pulls you, and it ain't the world that's wheeling no more, but you. But Mr. Frog, you're pretty calm. You're a bit like Ms. Toad, who stared at the moon with me that night in France not long ago. Calm, didn't mind me picking her up, us staring together. Same moon, different night, same feeling. Complete, but then that pull, moon tugging on all that water you pretend you don't got inside you, heart skipping a beat in wondering at all you ain't got to wondering 'bout lately.

What would that be like, Mr. Frog? That one there, not far, wheeling about the same pace as you, going up when you go up, both of you losing the ground. Not one arm crossed over the other, with one eye on the moon and one eye on me, not like you Mr. Frog, but maybe.

## *That Feeling Again, Mr. Frog*

Mr. Frog, I knew this'd happen. Big heart beating all slow, more time on this earth than you with the little hearts, but rushing around like I got a whole lot less. Sure don't got time to hang around awhile, sit on this beam and eat mosquitoes drunk on my blood when there's a world to stand on, the world what's forgetting its gravity, pulling the wrong way, up towards the moon like Ceridwen, and all that comes after.

There's that feeling again, Mr. Frog.

Goodnight.

# *The*
# *Summoning*

## I.

She walks in absentmindedly, lays her sword on the kitchen counter, and makes some tea. I didn't expect to see her so soon.

"So," I ask, my heart seizing up. "You're here."

"Hi!" she smiles, like it's fucking nothing. "Figured you'd need me."

I'm trying not to cringe. I know she can see this, and I know she won't say a word on it. "He's not…" She ignores me. She's sifting through the small plastic bags next to her sword.

"You went–oh! Good idea. How much they sell it for?"

She's taken the cap off. She's holding it to one nostril, holding the other shut with her knuckle, inhaling hard. Her eyes roll back in her head, she's in bliss, our private joke.

We both laugh.

"Six dollars. Put the cap back on, yeah?"

She answers my request with a sharp glance, rubs some of it under her neck, smiles, then twists the lid on. "Did you do that trick on him?"

I laugh. She's seen it before. Unclothed, wrestling flesh. A man licking my armpits, pulls back to stare at my face, his eyes wild lust and confusion–and it's time. I fumble for my boots where I've dumped the contents of my pockets, pull out the bottle. The label's fallen off long ago from the brown glass. He looks excited, I open it, I hold it to his nose.

"Wait–what the fuck?"

"Vetiver," I answer, smiling.

"I thought it was poppers."

"I know. Cool, huh?"

"Not yet," I answer her, the pain suddenly welling up. "If he texts, I'll…"

She puts the bottle down, unscrews the lid from a canning jar. "You're making a damiana chocolate liquer? Really? For me? You don't forget much."

I grunt a bit. "I'm glad you're changing the subject."

"I know!" she shouts, sifting through a paper bag, smelling everything. "That's why you love me." She pulls out a bag of herbs, spilling them everywhere.

"Fuck–I forgot to close that, sorry."

She smiles more. She doesn't say a thing about the bottle. "You went witch-shopping. Rough moon, huh?"

"Yeah," I sigh.

"Yeah," she replies, sighing too.

## II.

We take our tea outside in the summer heat. The air's getting thicker, soggy. Lightning flashes without thunder in the darkened sky to the south, though we're sitting in searing sun.

I smoke. She smokes. We ash into the grass, stare into the live oak strung with lamps like there's something else there to see. I spill my tea. She spills hers in solidarity. We say nothing, tracing the shadows on the bark with our eyes, letting our glances wander onto the lizards skirting through the mulch.

I haven't chain smoked since Berlin. Not since those nights in bars full of hip bearded shirtless guys, sweat glistening their chests and matting their fur, lithe but some with enough stomach that you wouldn't scrape your jaw nuzzling them with your chin. 2-for-1 beer nights, music I never recognized but loved, so much cigarette smoke I'd go to the basement darkroom for air. I suddenly want to smoke an entire pack again, a beer in the other hand, the music ripping my flesh as men press against me and smile, flirt, disappear again into the morass of dancing souls. Threads of attention caught on their forms, tugging me into them. And then the flick of a lighter and the thread flares and severs, and I am safe behind a cloud of smoke.

# Witches In A Crumbling Empire

She's feeling it too, indulges me. Nods, lights another. We're outside, so there's no ash to clear out later from keyboards, just like our cups make no tea-rings on the grass. Tendrils of smoke rise from the ends of our fags and hang in the heavy air.

She sighs.

I sigh.

The storm comes quick. We track wet grass with our bare feet across the floor, grab a glass of water, and hide in my room.

## III.

*What kind of underwear do you wear?*

I turn to her and grunt. "What kind of question is that?"

She shrugs. "He's hot though. Um, maybe they're trunks?"

I look at them. "They're sorta briefs," I tap out on the cracked screen of my phone. "But not."

"Take a picture," she whispers. She's reading over my shoulder.

I laugh nervously. "No. That's totally not me."

She's getting giddy. "...yet."

I growl. "Well, he hasn't asked for cock photos, and it's been like 14 messages. That's a good sign. It's kinda childish though."

"Right?" she nods, excited. "You're totally going to."

I don't really have the heart to protest. I text him back. "Uh…hold on."

## IV.

I stand in front of the mirror. It's awkward. The mirror is huge, but the sink gets in the way a bit. I take off my shirt, unbutton my fly, let my pants slide down my legs. I flex, and am a bit surprised at what I see. Also, a bit aroused. I turn around. "You see this?" She smiles and says nothing, but she's staring too, curious, amused. "I kinda feel like a goddess," I say, and it's such a strange way of putting it but it feels really good.

I flex some more. Weeks of hard exercise is doing some awesome shit to my already-huge legs. My arms and chest are still sore from lifting in the morning, so much so I'm having trouble holding the camera at the angle I want. I take a few, look back through the photos. They're not bad at all. Before I lose courage I send him a raw image.

*Oh wow I want to get naked with you dude now. Hot.*

She reads that and smiles. "See! But is he going to tell us what kind of underwear that is or what?"

*I want to take those trunks off and put your manhood in my mouth and feel you throb*

"Trunks," I tell her.

The guy texts again. He wants a date. Soon. He's also included detailed descriptions of what he'd like me to do to him.

I compose a reply. "Awesome. You can help me forget the boy who's ghosting me."

"Don't," she shouts, teasingly. "Unless he's got a fetish for forlorn poets, he'll never take those trunks off you in person."

## V.

She and I hang in my room for awhile. I play with the image, add a filter. I text one of my best friends. "I think I'm getting ghosted," I tell him. I send him the photo, and then add, "I think I am going to transform every silly boy emotion into a pound of muscle."

His reply is exactly what I needed:

*A time honored practice of masculinity. Looking good! Cute underwear.*

"You forgot to tell him they're trunks," she giggles.

Trunks. Yeah. Trunks. The same pair he yanked off me after several hours of some of the deepest conversation I'd had in a while. After the beers, after he introduced me to his rats, after all that time spent talking about magic, and meaning, and how neither of us want monogamy and wouldn't it be awesome if we spent a lot of time together before I go to France? All that emotion deeper even then my throat and his, a surface in tumult but far under it a peace, the quiet of the ocean floor. Funny that we both have Welsh names, funny that we'd worked the same jobs, funny that we fit together like bodies hewn from the same flesh.

Trunks and a shirt I didn't wash for two days because they smelled like him, a calm smell, the scent of quiet with base notes of ferocity. Trunks and a shirt I eventually washed, because the scent faded in the flood of texts from him, a flood I returned, so many on either side, such worded intensity throwing me happily off balance. Songs I don't listen to much became songs I listened to loudly and often, each helping to parse out and place the whelm of feelings.

Trunks, I guess, yeah. Trunks I bought s because all my clothes were old and ratty, because I had some extra cash, because I didn't need to look poor, because I wanted to see what new clothes felt like. And to the trunks I added shirts, and trousers, and later in Berlin suspenders. I was wearing these the night I spent with the goofy, hairy, beautiful London artist, gnawing on his cock for hours while we talked about art and life and cities. I was wearing these with the short, built Commie labor librarian who begged me to fuck him with such words saying no would have been silly. I was wearing these with the thuggish muscle-daddy who mentioned marriage after he came, with the hipster farmer on the border of Poland who ground his body into my cock so hard I thought it'd break. I was wearing these trunks the last night with-

## VI.

She and I are sitting, editing. Second draft of another's manuscript. I'm trying not to jump ahead to the formatting. I ask her indulgence, and she smiles. "Make it fucking pretty. You have time now."

"Ouch," I answer. "He's really ghosting me, isn't he?"

"Let's go smoke," she replies.

I was already reaching for them in my mind. She and I share the same thoughts. We stand in the darkness as frogs call, the burning red tip of lit cigarette flaring.

"You think?"

She puffs hard, exhales slowly, takes a minute to answer. "Funny to have your life all going how you hoped it would, to have had months of amazing sex and an ever-increasing awareness of your body, to find magic coursing through your flesh from someplace else and back again, to become a shapeshifter, to find peace, to sear through the cold memories of sorrow and find them melting into great wells of joy. Funny to feel the pull of your future tug so strong you want to tug back."

We look at each other.

I don't answer.

## VII.

We wake groggy. We were up 'till four editing. It felt amazing.

"I'm not working out today," I tell her, as she pours me a second cup of coffee.

"Okay! Can we have smoothies anyway, though?"

I laugh. I throw extra fruit in it, and coffee because why the fuck not? We do some work. I'm listless, though. I burn some incense, and then burn some more. I brew some damiana iced tea. I smoke a few too many cigarettes.

"I'm gonna text him," I tell her.

"Okay," she says. She rarely says no.

"Hey mate," I start.

"I, uh, am worried you might be ghosting me. And I wanted to tell you that regardless I'm happy we met, and I wish you deep joy."

"Add your name," she says.

"He knows my name. That makes it formal."

She stares at me and says nothing.

I stare at the screen.

I sigh.

"Be well. –Rhyd."

"Let's go smoke," she says.

"Okay," I nod, sombre. "And after that I need a nap."

## VIII.

Before I'm finished with the first cigarette, he's texted back.

*Um so, sorta awkward, things with me and another guy kind of intensified…*

We read the rest of his texts together. They feel good, honest. She helps me edit a reply back. She makes me delete "no worries" and "it's okay." I like when she's my editor; my replies feel honest, neither punishing nor coddling. Just really, really human.

## IX.

The guy who asked about my underwear texts too. I wait a little while on that reply to give myself space. She gives me some space too, quiet, staring at the bark of the live oak in the backyard.

"It needs more rosewater," I say to her. "And I think I'm gonna burn lots of incense today."

She nods.

I rub my chest some, talk to myself. I'm surprised at how it feels, stronger, flesh more solid than I've ever remembered. I let a few tears drop. They fall, she smiles. We celebrate together every moment of daring, every offer of love rebuffed.

She's good for this shit. She doesn't speak, just waits, lets me feel, feels with me.

## X.

I sit down at my desk. It's messy. Teacups, incense, random witch-bits and paper and cigarettes. Random bits from lovers, a lock of indigo hair, a cock ring, ticket stubs to the Sulis shrine in Bath. Candle-stubs, my wallet, grave dirt, feathers.

"I should clean this," I say.

She shakes her head. "You should write."

She's right. She usually is.

I light some incense and start to write. And then I laugh, thinking on all the witch-herbs I bought the day before.

"I summoned you, didn't I?" I ask, sipping tea as I type.

She shrugs, types some more, then adds:

No.

You summoned yourself.

# The Hunger
## of the Feed

*"One of your very suicidal friends has started a live video. Watch it before it ends..."*

I think it was the former co-worker popping pills while crying into her phone saying "good-bye" that finally broke me.

Not that hers was the first live suicide-attempt on Facebook I'd witnessed. Before her there was the bi-polar former lover: he always changed his profile picture to some scene from a Black metal album cover and quoted one-line lyrics as status updates before the walk to the bridge or the knife-blade to the wrists.

It wasn't just the real-time suicide attempts, though. It was also looking at the Facebook profile of the man I fucked three days after he got out of jail for meth-related crimes. Before the meth he was a Pagan leader, inspiring hundreds to go out into the woods and be primal animists communing again with the spirits of place and ancestor. Then the meth, then the prison, and when he gets out the comments on his update about being released?

"Hey bro woof glad u back on FB where u been?" and "Wat up hottie missed ur posts," as if his descent into pain and trauma were just another thing to "like" in The Feed.

It wasn't just that, or the suicides. It was also all the arguments with people I'll never meet. People who consider themselves in "community" with me but have none of the shared mutual existences that create community. "You're a transmisogynist" said someone who's never met me, "you're a gaslighting manarchist" said someone else. And then the social crusades following upon these comments, complete strangers with their trousers around their ankles sitting on toilets across the world demanding I apologize for some sentence in an essay they misread.

It was all that, I guess, but also something I've always known: The Feed wants. The Feed demands. And The Feed hungers.

## ...And Dwelt Among Us

As a Market arises in complexity, it begins to dominate each individual within it, inculcating its logic and demands into its participants. None of those participants have any say in what those logics and demands are; the agency of each is limited to binary choices: buy this or that, work here or there, but always buy and always work.

It is the same with a City. Though a community within it may attempt to influence policies and interactions in the sphere they inhabit, the City has its own logic, limiting any community's ability to fully wield power over their lives. A Black neighborhood can demand less-violent policing all they want, just as a white neighborhood might demand a greater focus on property crime; neither can hope to influence policing itself, only its aesthetic manifestations.

These greater logics, these egregoric demands, also inhabit the individuals which comprise it. This is why you cannot escape Capitalism: your rent is determined by Capital, your food is produced by capitalist modes of production, your wages are determined by capitalist manipulation of labor markets. Even if you lived unwaged, homeless, and only ate food out of trash cans, you are still limited by Capitalism, which also determines where you are allowed to live (all land is owned…), how much food is available in those dumpsters you dive, and how much the police are paid to imprison you for sleeping rough on private property or in "public" parks.

This inescapable logic makes each of us both subjects to Capitalism as well as re-producers of its logic. When we don't trespass or when we pay for groceries instead of stealing them, we re-inforce the sacrality of private property and the capitalist mode of production. When we buy anything, or pay for anything, or sell anything, we participate in this constant reproduction even if we do so in anti-capitalist ways.

As with The Market and The City, The Feed's own logics and own demands inhabit ours, reproduce themselves through the actions of each participant. These operations and these reproductions are obscured in the same way that the connections between the demands of Capitalism and our individual decisions within Capitalism are obscured. We cannot view the whole from the part, the forest from just one tree from which it is comprised.

A lone tree in a field exists differently from a tree within a forest. It need not compete with other trees for sunlight, but likewise does not benefit from the deep processes of decay and renewal which arise in forests. Not least of these processes are the fungal mats or mycelium which sometimes span thousands of acres, connecting entire forests within an organic communication network sometimes likened to human nervous systems. Trees within such networks seem to respond to each other through this network, slowing or increasing their growth in accordance to environmental changes elsewhere within the network.

Some have attempted to suggest such networks, organic and otherwise, are the origin of consciousness, or create a kind of consciousness. But "complexity theory" (or whatever the new pop-psych-science term is for it these days) is usually accompanied by the same sort of exuberant utopianism that predicts an impending Singularity or an end to war and poverty, scientists drunk on what the Age of Aquarius idiots were drinking decades ago.

We were also promised jetpacks and assured that globalizing Capitalism would make Africa wealthy, propaganda all of it. So we don't need to propose that mycelium networks and social networks are the precursors to consciousness. Simpler materialist parallels are sufficient to show that The Feed affects the individuals within it in similar ways and changes their behaviors to operate in tandem.

## Genuflecting At The Altar

The selfie is the perfect example of this, but not the selfie itself. Here I do not speak of the images littering social networks (I've plenty, by the way), but the human act of the selfie. Remove the meaning-content of the selfie (the image itself) and instead consider the human actions which produce the image: humans with an arm extended, their heads trained on a rectangle in their hand, their heads usually slightly tilted. They then smile at the rectangle and then put it away.

The selfie has cultural content, of course, and it is not done randomly. Only at certain times and during certain conditions do humans extend their arms and smile at a rectangle. One needs first own a rectangle, and then experience the correct conditions during which the individual divines the correct time for the behavior.

The moment of the selfie is individually-determined, certainly, but the imperative of the selfie is collective. In this way, though, the human actions of the selfie start to sound a lot more similar to religious behavior such as genuflection or prayer: one crosses themselves at certain moments determined by individual decisions, but crossing oneself is a thing one does because one is Catholic.

The Feed (social networks in general) can be said to affect the material conditions and actions of those within it in the same way that Catholicism does. Though one might be likely to object that Catholicism has ideological and religious content while Twitter, Facebook, Instagram, and all the rest appear to have none, such an objection misses the materialist perspective. The content of Catholicism (or any other religious or ideological system) obscures its material existence. The Catholic Church is a network of hundreds of thousands of churches, charities, properties, missions, hospitals, and agencies funded by donations from participants and headed by priests, bishops, cardinals, and a pope; this is its material reality, its physical structure through which political, religious, cultural, and ideological content is distributed and reproduced by Catholics who have no real influence or power over what content is actually distributed.

It is the same with The Feed. We are parishioners in the Holy Church of Facebook, reproducing behaviour-as-content (taking selfies, writing posts, sharing tweets, clicking reactions) which The Feed distributes according to its own logic (Facebook's deeply-obscured algorithm). And like the devoted at Mass, we passively take in what the priests have transubstantiated by occulted processes we can only accept, not engage in ourselves.

To what purpose, though? Because at least with religions we feel we can divine the motives of the priests; with Social Media there is no published doctrine nor sacred texts we can sort through. For such an answer, we need yet again use a materialist framework and ask not "what do they believe?" but "what are its effects on us?" Here a recent essay from Slavoj Zizek gives us more clarity:

> ...to understand how our lives are regulated today, and how this regulation is experienced as our freedom, we have to focus on the shadowy relation between private corporations which control our commons and secret state agencies. We shouldn't be shocked at China but at ourselves who accept the same regulation while believing that we retain our full freedom and the media just help us to realize our goals (while in

*China people are fully aware that they are regulated). The biggest achievement of the new cognitive-military complex is that direct and obvious oppression is no longer necessary: individuals are much better controlled and "nudged" in the desired direction when they continue to experience themselves as the free and autonomous agents of their own life...*

In a word, the doctrine of The Feed is control. And one need not delve very deep to find proof of how much control over human behavior they already wield: we can start by noting (with wonder and awe) the millions of people daily standing with their arms extended in public places, staring at a rectangle and smiling, in order to feed The Feed with a digital reproduction of their face. Because of a physical network of corporations, servers, electronics manufacturers, and a vast army of technological workers, we take selfies. What seems like a "free and autonomous" act of individual agency is, like all our actions within capitalist markets, determined by an external logic over which we have neither control nor influence. And again like capitalist markets or the Catholic Church (and unlike mycelium or other organic networks), there are central authorities which rule over these logics and demands.

Indeed, the logics and demands are theirs. We, participants in The Feed, merely enact, fulfill, manifest, and reproduce those desires. The live-feed suicide attempt of my friend manifested their will, just as all the twitter-battles and internet social justice wars also reproduce their logic. They shape us into devoted citizens of the world they create, ensuring we do not stray too far from the flock and are never led into temptation or delivered into evil by dangerous ideas they helpfully prevent us from seeing.

I don't know how this will end, what more they will change in us, nor can I foresee any hope of escape. Just as there is no market outside the dominance of capital, there is no dissemination of ideas outside of social media any longer: when this essay is done it will go into The Feed along with all the effluvia of our social production. Perhaps it will appear for you below a selfie or a cute kitten photo, just above a stranger's complaints about their job or loveless marriage, somewhere near an ad for a product you don't need and a listicle about how you are being oppressed.

Maybe it'll even appear along with a live feed of a friend's suicide attempt. Be sure to watch it before it ends.

# A New Luddite Rebellion

"Welcome to the modern world. It's just like the old world, except it doesn't work."

-Peter Grey

My friend and I were both hungry; me perhaps a bit more so since I'd been traveling all day, hadn't eaten that morning and it was now mid-evening.

"I'll take you to dinner," I told him. "Somewhere close–maybe pizza."

"Okay," he answered, and then started looking at his phone. "This place has really good reviews. Just need to take two trains."

I was really hungry. "How long will that take?" I asked.

"45 minutes, maybe an hour."

I shook my head. "Seems far and will cost a lot to get there. Isn't there a place nearby?"

It was his turn to shake his head. "None with good reviews."

"I don't care," I answered, probably a bit too curtly. The hunger was irritating me greatly. "Let's just walk to one of them."

So we did, set out into the cold city night, finally coming to an Italian restaurant. I looked at the menu, the prices were decent. "Perfect," I said, turning to him.

"I can't find any reviews on Trip Advisor though," he answered. "But there's one about a mile from here with a lot of reviews…"

Exhausted and frustrated, I snapped back: "Food's food. I'm buying anyway…let's go in."

"But it might not be good," he replied, until suddenly seeing something on his phone that made him excited. "Nevermind, I found it. Good reviews, we can go in."

I've thought about this interaction very often since it happened a few months ago. My friend isn't stupid; in fact, he's very intelligent, and his magical insights into the world are often quite profound. Nor is he hardly alone in succumbing to the peculiar sort of paralysis of inaction I've recounted here. In fact, I suffer from it often too, as no doubt you likely do.

The desire to know if something is good before you try it, to want certainty about the uncertain–that's hardly a new thing. But what is new, deeply radically new, is our reliance on social media (and the corporations which run them) and technological devices to give us that certainty, to tell us it's going to be okay, to remove the risk that an action might not result in the absolute best conditions.

As with a night out at a restaurant or a date with a person met online, so too with any of the actions we might take towards revolution. We look to Tumblr and Twitter to gauge the sentiment of others, to divine if our groups and theories and plans are popular enough, have all the required sign-off's from every possible identity focus-group, and nod sagely when told 'that won't work' by whichever correctly-branded social justice personality happened to come through our feed that particular minute.

We do not revolt because we might fail. People might get shot or imprisoned, vulnerable people might suffer more than they already do, police oppression might increase, and all that effort could be wasted forever. And though these fears have always been good fears, our reliance on technology for re-assurances of certainty has amplified our inaction. This is not a controversial statement: if many of us can barely try a new restaurant without relying on smartphones to take away the very minimal risk of an awful meal, why would we expect ourselves to face actual, real risk?

## Those Satanic Mills

If you feel this way of critiquing technology seems bizarre, anti-modern, primitive, or appears to ignore all the good that technology has done, you might be tempted to describe all this as "Luddite." And you'd be correct, and not in the ways most moderns have come to understand what the Luddites fought for.

The Luddites have always fascinated me. Men and women, sometimes cross-dressing, stealing into oppressive factories in the middle of the night to smash looms to stop production: that's quite hardcore, regardless of why they did it. Besides the awesome acts of industrial sabotage, two other aspects of what the followers of King (or Ned, or Captain) Ludd did two hundred years ago are extremely relevant to us now.

The first aspect is their anarcho-Paganism. They all claimed to follow a ghostly captain or leader who urged them on their night-time strikes against the industrialists. The stories they told about exactly who he was varied just as often as their actions: Ludd lived under a hill, or in a well, or under a church, all three places not ironically located "somewhere" in Sherwood forest, where Robin of Locksley and his fellow rogues were said to hide. Ludd was a spirit, a king, or a general ("No General But Ludd/Means The Poor Any Good" went one of their chants), or just a captain amongst them, or even the ghost of a man named Ned Ludd (killed after sabotaging a factory, goes the stories). Like other similar groups such as the Whiteboys and Molly Maguires and Rebeccas, the Luddites invoked the mythic against capitalists and the State to great effect, at least while their resistance lasted.

And that brings me to the third aspect of the Luddite resistance, the part which I find most haunting as another year on this earth passes for me (I'm 41 today, it seems). To explain this aspect, though, we need to step back a bit and look not just at the Luddites themselves but at the era in which they fought and the strange (and eerily familiar) historical circumstances which created the world around them.

If industrial Capitalism has a specific birthdate and birthplace, it was 1769 in Preston, Lancashire. It was in that year and in that place the very first modern factory was built by Richard Arkwright. The sound of the factory was compared to "the devil's bagpipes," a fact memorialized in this poem by Lorna Smithers:

> When Richard Arkwright played the devil's bagpipes on Stoneygate a giant hush came over the town. The blistering whirring sound against the pink horizon of a sun that would not set over clear sights for two centuries of soot and smog was damnable. Yes damnable! Gathering in storm clouds over Snape Fell.
>
> You who have seen a premonition might have heard the village seers tell of smoke for flesh charry knees and the squalor of shanty towns. Red brick mills turning satanic faces to the coin of their heliotropic sun: Empire.

*Piecers running between generations bent legged beggers, tongue in cheek defiant.
Weavers watching shuttles slipping through fingers like untamed flies. Luddites sweeping
across greens with armaments and gritted teeth...*

It took forty years for Arkwright's new terror, "those Satanic mills" as
William Blake called them in 1804, to finally spark the resistance movement
known as the Luddites. In that space of time, Arkwright's first mill multi-
plied into 2400 similar factories spread throughout England (mostly in the
major cities), an average of 60 a year.

So, in two generations, Britain had gone from a place where there was
no such thing as a factory to a place where there were several thousands. In
four decades, an entire society which had started out knowing nothing
about industrialization appeared to become irrevocably industrialised, and it
was at that point the Luddites struck.

But why then? Why not before? And why fight what appeared to be
inevitable?

## Against the Modern World

We must first ignore the modern interpretation of what a Luddite is.
They weren't anti-technology, nor slow-to-adapt old people hopelessly left
behind in a new world. Nor were they only concerned with fighting for
better wages for weavers (who, before the factories, were able to support
themselves and large families on the income from their specialized trade).

They were people close to my age and somewhat younger, the oldest
people alive in Britain who could still remember the old world before
factories, but still also young enough to actually work in them. They were a
generation that stood on a threshold between the pre-industrial world and
the new industrial capitalist order.

Imagine if you will what it must have been like to see your parents and
the older people in your villages, towns, and cities starving because they
could not or would not adapt to this brave new world. Many of them were
too old, feeble, or weak-sighted to work in the factories, and anyway the
factory owners preferred children as young as five to do much of the
nimble work (and they couldn't fight back). So while you see the older
generation starving and destitute, you also see your own children or
younger siblings coming home from the mills with broken fingers, strange
bruises, and unmentionable wounds from their 14-hour day crawling under machinery to tie broken threads or retrieve loose bobbins.

And then there's you, you and others your age, still young enough to
work in many of the mills yet old enough to remember when the world
wasn't like this at all.

# Witches In A Crumbling Empire

Now, it is almost impossible for us to imagine a world before factories, even as in many modern Liberal Democratic countries very few of us have actually stepped foot in one. That's not because they aren't around anymore: they've moved mostly to Asia and Africa, where exhausted workers are crammed up like cattle in a slaughterhouse to make the phone and laptops you're probably reading this on (as well as the clothes you're wearing, possibly the chair you're sitting on, and most of the stuff inside the home where you lay your head at night) for little or no wages.

And it is almost impossible to imagine what society was like before the factory. What was it like to only wear clothes made by yourself or people who lived nearby? What was life like before the cities swelled with displaced peasants blinking in the light of dawn before the gates of textile and steel mills, hungry and exhausted but jostling each other in line for a job that day to feed their family? What did the streets and town squares look like at night before everyone had to wake up at dawn to go to work? How did we relate to each other before wages became the only way to survive? And what did society look like before mass-production, when no one ever wore the same thing, when pre-packaged experiences, monoculture, and conformity were literally impossible?

It is almost impossible to imagine the world before factories. Almost, but not completely. Because we are living in a similar world to what the Luddites experienced

## "All that is sacred is profaned..."

If you can pinpoint any places in western history where technology severely altered the way human society functioned, I suspect there are three. The most obvious one is the industrial revolution, which was also the birth of Capitalism. The one before that changed the world as well (but much more slowly) was the invention of the printing press, which gave to early merchants and the bourgeoisie the power to disseminate literature outside the strictures of religious and royal decree. And while we tend to see that invention as a net gain for humanity, we must remember that mass-printing and distribution has always been primarily in the hands of the rich, with the rest of us merely passive consumers.

The third—well, that's the era we're in now, the computer/internet "revolution." The first node-to-node digital communication happened in 1969, 200 years after from the birth of Richard Arkwright's steam-powered looming frame. But being military technology, it took more than a decade for that technology to filter out to non-military capitalists and become the

A New Luddite Rebellion

"World Wide Web." In the following decades, we've gone from a world where random ("risky") human interactions occurred only in public spaces to one where most such interactions now occur online.

We don't need to dig very far to understand that this technological change has radically altered what it means to be a human in a capitalist society. For instance: before cellphones, you could only be reached at home. That meant if you needed to wait for a call you had to stay by the phone, but it also meant that your life was less likely to revolve around the ability of someone to get a hold of you immediately. There was no expectation that your attention could be gotten at any hour of the day because such a thing was impossible.

Before texting and email there were letters. You had to take the time to decide what you were going to say to someone, write it out on paper, post it in the mail, and then wait some amount of time for a reply. Thus human interactions were slower and more ponderous and most of all more intentional. Even the angriest of letters wouldn't arrive until the next day at the earliest, and this slowness meant there was always at least a little time to re-think your immediate fury, unlike now with our instantaneous send buttons.

Social media, however, probably represents the largest shift in how we relate to each other and also how we see ourselves. To have large groups of friends you had to do stuff for them, and with them, call them on weekends or send them letters, catch up with them for coffee or go to their parties or invite them for dinner, take vacations to see them or host them in your home. Now you need only post an update and read theirs to feel you've performed acts of friendship.

Accompanying that shift has been an increasing feeling of isolation and alienation. So many people now self-diagnose with introversion (as with trauma, or social anxiety, or many other ailments) that one wonders how humans ever managed to talk to each other before the internet.

The general response to this apparent increase in alienation is to state it has always been there, that being connected to each other more via the internet has helped us talk about it more, and that anyway we are #Blessed the internet came around to let us all be social despite our fear and misanthropy.

But in this case particularly, those of us who stand on the same threshold of change that the Luddites also stood upon cannot help but remember: we all did fine without social media. Better, even. We got over our shyness and anxiety because we had to, and the internet appears to have merely enabled us to not get over such things, to not address our social anxiety and fear of rejection and instead hide safely behind a screen.

Before the internet, binge-watching television ("Netflix and chill") or staring at a screen for hours a day was a sign you'd given up on yourself and the world around you, were depressed and really just needed a friendly face or to go for a walk. They were symptoms of serious depression, indications that some large issue in your life has been unaddressed for too long and the things to "get you through" had become addictions which prevented you from seeking help.

Now those things are all proud marks of "self-care" enabled by technology without which we'd all surely be miserable, lonely humans. Nevermind that we are still miserable, lonely humans, and probably more so now.

## Non-Binary Poly Radical #Blessed Vegan Cruelty-Free #Resister Queer Theorist Influencers Unite!™

Less controversial but even more unaddressed is what this new technological revolution has done to our ability to survive, to earn enough money to eat and pay rent. The much-vaunted and ridiculous "internet of things" has made it so we rarely get to 'own' the things we pay capitalists for, and must re-sell parts of ourselves constantly in order to compensate for dwindling wages and no savings. This is the curse of the "millenial" (a marketing term that, like so much else, somehow became a "fact" in capitalist society)–to have no steady income but to have thousands of Instagram followers in the hopes of one day having enough to be an "influencer." To face insurmountable college debt and no way to secure housing but to get thousands of retweets on Twitter.

It is not just the fate of millenials. I've had two posts shared over 100,000 times and one seen by 1.5 million people. And yet I haven't been able to afford eating more than twice a day in years, and have been nomadic for the last five years because 1.5 million views doesn't pay rent.

The answer to the poverty experienced by more and more people (again–not just millenials) is to 'monetize' your life. Or as put in a rather brilliant essay about nomads like myself at It's Going Down (*"Living In A Van Down By The Instagram"*):

*The point here is not to whine about how we all can't be special snowflakes or social media super-stars; the point is to state that capital is colonizing all aspects of our lives, including online worlds, and attempting to make us in turn generate profit, content, and value during all waking moments, either online or off. And, there's no better backdrop to do this than when we are constantly traveling, as we in turn are utilizing and activating our social networks for the sake of monetizing them. Thus, we are pushed to take photos and tag corporations in the hopes that maybe one day we could get $50 for a sponsored post. To fundamentally turn ourselves, and our lives, into brands.*

*As was pointed out in the new book, Now, by the Invisible Committee, this has become both the economic baseline as well as central anxiety of our time. We aren't just driving somewhere and enjoying a podcast or randomly picking up a hitch hiker, we are instead missing out on an opportunity to sell our labor power for Uber or Lyft. We aren't taking photos to share with loved ones, we are building up our brand and trying to gain followers, which we will then sell to multinational corporations. This is the logic of the gig economy applied to all aspects of our lives, at all times, and in all scenarios.*

To monetize yourself, though, requires you make yourself more sell-able, becoming a brand, a product, constantly adapting to market demands. Or as Badean wrote in *"Identity In Crisis,"* in the *Journal of Queer Nihilism:*

*The collapse of traditional subject positions is managed through the proliferation of new positions: app designers, graphic designers, cyber sex workers, queer theorists, feminist publishers, social network engineers, trend hunters, eBay sellers, social justice activists, performance artists, porn directors, spammers, party promoters, award winning baristas.*

*We are forced to continually define ourselves, to enact countless operations upon ourselves so as to produce ourselves anew each day as someone worth taking to market — our basic survival depends on the ceaseless deployment of increasingly discreet technologies of the self.*

*Everything is for sale: our sex appeal, our fetishes, our tattoos, our radicalism, our fashion sense, our queerness, our androgyny, our fitness, our fluidity, our abnormality, our sociability. Facebook and Twitter function as the new resume.*

*We are caught in the unending necessity to be continually educating, training, exploring, perfecting, and fine-tuning ourselves. Our continual self-invention is both economic imperative and economic engine.*

No doubt this seems dire enough, but one more dark truth emerges from this constant race. Because if we are constructing our identities in order to become more sale-able to people (be that for money or Facebook likes or even just to be noticed in this new hyper-gendered micro-radical hierarchy of new identities), how do we even know who we are anymore?

To be honest, I don't always know. I am a radical queer anarchist pagan nomad punk fag brother boyfriend theorist bard druid, but none of that actually tells me what I am, only the hashtags people might use to define me on a social media post. Labels that once gave meaning now become indelible brandings. Try to shift any of those identities and the world (or the social media world, anyway) pushes back...hard. And just as often, those labels themselves are fiercely contested: I cannot count how many times I've been told I'm too "masculine-presenting" to be allowed to use the term queer.

So who am I? Who gets to decide? And why are we using capitalist tools to mediate those discussions in the first place? Or is it possible it's those very tools which have triggered these crises in the first place?

## Not All Revolutions Are Good

*The bourgeoisie cannot exist without constantly revolutionising the instruments of production, and thereby the relations of production, and with them the whole relations of society. Conservation of the old modes of production in unaltered form, was, on the contrary, the first condition of existence for all earlier industrial classes. Constant revolutionising of production, uninterrupted disturbance of all social conditions, everlasting uncertainty and agitation distinguish the bourgeois epoch from all earlier ones. All fixed, fast-frozen relations, with their train of ancient and venerable prejudices and opinions, are swept away; all new-formed ones become antiquated before they can ossify. All that is solid melts into air, all that is holy is profaned, and man is at last compelled to face with sober senses his real conditions of life, and his relations with his kind.*

*(The Communist Manifesto)*

The shift wrought by internet technology wherein identity is now the very battlefield of our ability to survive in the world may seem utterly different from any other struggle which has come before. In context of the struggle the Ludditesc and the early communists and anarchists fought, however, not much has really changed.

The rise of industrial apitalism triggered vast shifts in social relations which are to this day still being constantly disrupted. It should thus be no surprise to us that "disruptive technology" is a statement of pride for many of the new architects of this current upheaval, an upheaval in which we also take part when we celebrate the destruction of older forms of relating (binary gender, hetero-normative society, class-based politics). What "good" comes from these disruptions unfortunately seems fleeting and probably is. Because while it is a beautiful thing that acceptance of gender variance and queer sexuality have become so prominent, it's a sick joke to say a poor queer or trans person desperately trying to pay rent by sleeping on a friend's couch while letting out their bedroom on AirBnb, turning tricks on

TaskRabbit or bareback hookup apps, and desperately looking for the perfect filter to get their Instagram account another 100 followers has somehow had their life "improved" by these disruptions.

Yet, to this current horror in which we all find ourselves, perhaps the Luddites might shrug and say, "at least you didn't have time forced upon you." Because along with the disruption of the factory from hand-craft and laborer to factory and wage-slave came the beginning of an oppressive order of time.

Clocks became no longer curiosities but requirements. Suddenly, knowing if it was half-past eight or just morning became the crucial difference between feeding your family for a day or starving on the street. Time literally had to be disciplined into us during the birth of industrialization, often times by Christian moralists like John Wesley working on behalf of the factory owners. Time became something that you "spent" rather than something that passed, work became measured not by what needed doing according to the season but what the factory boss demanded you do within a set number of hours.

Before industrialization, work was task-oriented. You planted at some times of the year, harvested at others, ground wheat and fixed carts, wove cloth and made clothes not when an arbitrary number declared it was "time" to do so but when the thing itself needed doing. And work itself was determined by how long you wanted to take doing the task, not how many hours the boss said you needed to stand at a counter or else be fired.

When attempting to imagine what that world was like (not very long ago), we tend to imagine it only for ourselves, what our own life might have been like. Harder to imagine, however, is what all of society itself was like without clocks as over-seers. Imagine then what life would be like if not just you but all your friends and all the people in your town lived life without clocks, and you get a little closer to understanding precisely what the Luddites were fighting for.

## A New Luddite Rebellion

It was against such radical, world-altering shifts that the Luddites broke into factories at night, smashing looms. One imagines they wanted their time back, they wanted their children and parents back, wanted the ability to survive without working in factories back. They wanted back the rich texture of a society where you knew the people who made your clothes, talked to the people who grew your food, or were those people themselves.

# Witches In A Crumbling Empire

We are living in another such time. People older than me lived most of their childhoods without the internet and do not (or cannot) adapt to a world where everything about them is on display, sold piecemeal through Facebook updates and Instagram photos.

Those much younger than me do not know a world without cell-phones, do not remember that it was possible to make new friends and meet amazing lovers without connecting first to an always-on device in your pocket. How many of them know you can arrive by train to a foreign city with just a paper map and a notebook and have the best trip of your life? How many will ever get a chance to experience what it was like to not just survive but actually have a pretty decent life in a city on less than full-time, barely-above minimum wage as I did in Seattle 15 years ago? And most of all, how many of them will ever know that risk and uncertainty is not something to be avoided at all costs but very often the thing which makes life worth living in the first place?

I barely remember what that was like.

I also barely remember what it was like to be anonymous, to have hours and hours of free time without devices I felt like I needed always to be looking at, constantly notifying me that emails and texts and retweets and messages are coming in. To have long conversations with strangers while waiting for a bus, to make new friends on the walk to work or find an awesome lover by chance while whiling away the day at a cafe. And most of all, I barely remember what it was like to know who I am without labels–to not need to call myself anything but my name, and have that be enough.

I want that all back. If you are close in age to me, you probably do to. If you are younger than me and don't know what that was like, perhaps my telling of it is enough to entice you to want it also, and if you are older than me you might be shaking your head, having already mourned what's been lost.

More than anything, we need this all back. Not just our time (consumed constantly by always-on devices and relentless updates). Not just our Selves (boxed in, categorized, labeled and shelved by any number of identities.). Not just our ability to pay rent and eat and still have enough money left over to enjoy the ever-dwindling number of months and days we have on this earth. Not just all that, but we need our will back, our reckless desire to act in the face of risk and uncertainty, the chaotic and unscripted interactions between ourselves and the world which make our lives not just exciting, but mythic.

And therein's the key to the ritual invocation we must perform to take back what we've watched slowly sold off of our lives with each new screech of the devil's bagpipes. There are spirits, gods, and ancestors who keep the memory of the old worlds even as we forget. Ludd was one, and though his followers failed to stop the horror born of the factories in England, some of us still remember their attempt. Be it Ludd or the Raven King, Brighid or Dionysos, or perhaps all the old gods and heroes summoned together, we can make another go at stopping this new horror waking upon the world. From the shattered remains of the past we can reconstruct a new resistance against this increasingly senseless drive towards self-as-product.

And if we fail, we will no doubt be smeared by many for being 'anti-modern' just as the Luddites were, dismissed and forgotten by many others, but definitely remembered by some, just as the Luddites are still remembered now.

We may indeed fail. The risks are very, very great, and there's no Trip Advisor listing to assure us that there will be good food and pleasant ambiance after our uprising. Perhaps our failures will be re-tweeted across the world, Facebook Live videos streaming our defeat to countless millions using greasy thumbs to scroll through the comments. We'll lose Instagram followers and potential Influencer sponsorships while the rich and powerful of the world destroy more forests, gun down more poor people, and start more wars.

We probably won't win. But I'm gonna try anyway, because I want my life back.

And maybe you do, too.

# Awakening Against What's Awakened

Berlin is a city of the dead. You hear them behind the raucous laughter in the clubs, in the space between stones on crowded streets. They're loudest especially in the time just after sunset, the gloaming, when Berlin seems suddenly to waken into life hidden from view of the day.

You know what happened to Berlin, probably. You know of the great conflagration in the souls of millions which suddenly turned all the minds of many towards the slaughter of a few. The parades through streets celebrating a new thing awakened, the shattered windows and bloodied faces. The seized printing-presses, the new flags adorning old stone. And then the deportations, and then the murders.

Some great Authority awakened into the world, and millions complied with its will.

## The Cries of the Dead

Often, it's easier to hear the dead than it is to hear the gods. Gods don't leave corpses to rot in alleyways, or journals to account their worlds. We may speak of the gods, and to them, but they exist in the realm of the pre-literate, the Abyss before human meaning. Any words we ascribe to them is mere translation, any relics bearing their name were made or invoked by us, not by them.

The dead, though—they leave books and buildings, papers and clothing, hair and bone and graffiti. Their bodies rot into the soil, feeding the harvests of our present. They leave words and warnings, their echoed screams shape the sense of a place. They plant trees under which we sit decades later, along a canal they built a century ago. Their impassioned groans and throes birthed those whose later orgasmic exhalations called into being the living who jog past me as I write.

The not-human dead are easier to see, though apparently mute. The cows whose skin binds my pants to my waist and shods my feet have not yet decomposed into the Abyss, but they did not in life speak a language I understand. The dead tree whose wood forms this bench upon which I sit may have once towered over villages from which Jews were hauled into camps, but its voice is silent in response to my questions.

It's from the dead that we even know of the gods, and the dead still speak. But I do not like what they have to say. The dead keep telling me about that great thing awakened, warning of another.

Something's happening.

One dead haunting me a bit particularly has been Walter Benjamin. Benjamin was born in Berlin. Feared more than anything returning there, hid in Paris, then Marseilles, as a nation inhabited by some strange new spirit swept through Europe, building camps into which their enemies were concentrated, then sacrificed. Even climbing a mountain gave him no quarter, as respect for the new religion had spread even to Spain.

## The Wotanic Spirit

I use the words "spirit" and "religion" without flippancy here, without metaphor. In a speech before the second world war broke out, Jung spoke of a Wotanic spirit awakening in Germany. The God of the German Christians seemed no longer the same God of the French Christians, no longer the same God which held together the imagined community of (Christian) Europe. An older god, an ancestral god, a god of dirt and blood, a god of rage and fear had arisen, dethroning the God of Civilization.

> *We are always convinced that the modern world is a reasonable world, basing our opinion on economic, political, and psychological factors. But if we may forget for a moment that we are living in the year of Our Lord 1936, and, laying aside our well-*

*meaning, all-too-human reasonableness, may burden God or the gods with the responsibility for contemporary events instead of man, we would find Wotan quite suitable as a casual hypothesis....*

*Perhaps we may sum up this general phenomenon as Ergriffenheit — a state of being seized or possessed. The term postulates not only an Ergriffener (one who is seized) but, also, an Ergreifer (one who seizes). Wotan is an Ergreifer of men, and, unless one wishes to deify Hitler-- which has indeed actually happened — he is really the only explanation.*

Jung's speech has some significant problems, not least of which is his linkage of the German people's physical ancestry–as well as culture–as a site for the awakening of a god. But the matter of the Ergriffenheit, the possession, mirrors plenty of other writers' descriptions of the strange spirit which seemed to inhabit those who fell under the sway of the Nazis.

But was it Wotan? Can a god do that? And anyway, what is is a god?

There's a theory that many of the gods we now know were all once humans. Odin, for instance, is thought to have been a powerful shaman-type figure, Brân was once a chieftain of the Belgii, Ceridwen and the Morrígan and Hecate once renowned and feared witches. After their deaths, their significant deeds were remembered through story, and over generations (centuries) the veneration people from who only knew them through these great tales made them divine.

Such an idea makes a lot of sense, judging from the last few millennia. Plenty of emperors, kings, and spiritual leaders have all been made into gods—often while they still lived. Even into the late 1700's in Europe, the touch of a royal was though to heal sickness.

In most of these instances, it was the persons themselves who made the revelation, declaring to their followers their true nature. Others, though, were made sacred after their deaths by religious leaders—though saints are subordinate to the God of the Catholics, sainthood elevates them over the realm of mere mortals. Their existence persists long after their deaths, reminded to us by venerations and sacred stories.

Were the Pagan gods maybe the same?

We cannot know when Odin was first known to those who claimed him as a god, nor whether the first to speak his name knew him as a god, a shaman, a chief, or something else entirely. And though this theory itself is neutral as to whether or not the gods-once-human are now gods, it has some uncomfortable implications for anyone who might now claim themselves a priest or mystic of such divine beings.

Jung may have been aware of this idea as he crafted his archetypal theory of the gods. But being no political theorist, Jung does not look directly at the way a State seems to inhabit the people the same way a god might.

## Gods Are Things

I should first explain what I even mean by gods. And for this I must first speak of trees.

Trees are a thing. They exist, as much as anything exists. And they are a thing almost every one of us will experience at least once.

Forget you have eyes for a moment and consider the experience of a tree. If you do not see them, you can still know there is a thing there by listening to the sound the wind makes through their branches, feeling the cool of their shade on a hot day, smelling the earthy decay of their leaves in late autumn or the fragrance of their blossoms in spring, tasting their fruit or their sap. You may know them even though they are dead, sitting upon a wooden bench or hearing the crinkle of newspaper, tasting alder or hickory on grilled meat or smelling the smoke from winter chimneys.

Trees are a thing you can experience, and probably have already. But how is a tree even a thing at all? Without witnessing the suspension of orange from branch, without seeing chopped wood set alight, how do you connect the ripe flesh of fruit or the warmth of a fireplace to the tree as thing? A pear is a thing, a pine coffin is a thing, toilet paper is a thing, but how are they then also part of a tree as thing?

Humans are also a thing. I feel a human when he touches my shoulder, my chest. I smell a human when she is near me, the mix of her sweat and perfume warmed by the heat of her body. I taste a human when he kisses me, when I lick his skin. And I hear humans when I walk through cities, when they shout at me or call my name.

Like a tree, I also feel what humans do even when they are not there. I walk across the cobbles they've lain, I sleep on the beds they've built, I eat the food they've grown. I choke on the fumes of their cars, I smell the dinners they cook as I pass windows thrown open to the summer air.

My knowledge of humans (like that of trees) comes from my senses. When I hear a human, my ears are resonating with the waves of sound their actions make. When I see them, my eyes discern the patterns of light which reflect off them. My nose and tongue translate the particulates kicked up from their existence, the nerves in my skin explode electric currents to my brain when their bodies press against mine. All this, too, is true for trees.

# Witches In A Crumbling Empire

We walk through a world swirling with the chaos of other things sharing it with us. We're all said to exist, to be, but we don't really have a good reason for being certain of that. We mostly just accept it on faith—and then forget there was anything to accept in the first place. We can't go around questioning our senses all the time. We'd never get around to living.

That acceptance is the gate to the world of meaning, the gate out of The Abyss of the rawest of life. Walking through that gate, we enter a great world enclosed by the earth itself, drenched and soaked in the meaning we weave from all the threads of the material. But we must be clear: it's we who do that weaving. We are the meaning-makers.

I experience the gods with the same senses through which I experience everything else, and call them things. Sometimes I feel a hand on the back of my neck, breath in my ear. That's Brân. Sometimes I see a pattern of light on water or the taste of something electric on the wind; that's Arianrhod. Flames dancing in a certain way, the scent of a home I haven't known yet, the lightest of rain on bare skin: Brighid. A sudden chill that awakens the body, the heightened alertness when the moon's a sharp crescent is when I smell Ceridwen, though the pattern of black branches in that same moonlight is Gwyn Ap Nudd.

One sharp taste on a tongue is called salt, a sweeter one is called sugar; these are just names, but names we're all quite insistent upon as being connected to things. Though a Frenchwoman would call the latter *sucre* and the former *sel*, a German insist *Salz* for the first and *Sukar* for the second, we're pretty attached to our own names for these things..

I'm pretty attached to the names I have for the experiences-called-gods, too. Though sometimes I use other names:. Brighid is the Lady of the Hearth, though sometimes of the Flame, or of Tears, or the Rain. Brân's the Raven King, and also the Guardian at the Gate of the Dead. Ceridwen's sometimes the Huntress, and sometimes Gwyn Ap Nudd Hunts too.

Arianrhod's the Silver Wheel, and a lot of other names I don't really understand yet. She avoids comprehension more than the others. When a lover bit my nipples until they started to bleed, I understood something about her I still don't get but feel again sometimes. When I see that pattern of light-on-water, I know a part of my mind awakens and understands. It just refuses to explain to the rest of me.

## Gods On Thrones

Gods occupy a space of human meaning. When something strange happens, fortuitous or synchronistic, and when that happens to co-incide with what I generally ascribe to the activity of the gods, I am connecting something to the gods by a thread called Meaning. Light dances on water a certain way and I think of Arianrhod. My consciousness seems to both to expand and yet become more porous into the land around me and I think Brân.

But the gods occupy a different space from other things to which we connect meaning. We usually call that place "Sacred," rather than mundane or normal. When I pour out offerings to Arianrhod, it's a sacred thread of meaning, a sort of special category of meaning set apart from all the others. And though we tend to think of that sacred as out of reach of the political, it's never been the case.

Kings, emperors, chiefs, and other human authorities have always ruled by the blessing of the divine, be that gods, God, or another sacred realm outside the reach of material influence. In the present, governments gain consent to rule by the will of the people; 500 years ago, kings ruled by the will of God and the blessing of the Church; in non-Christian areas, kings claimed to rule through the blessing of the land or the gods.

That authorial space the sacred occupies in political realms is also a realm of meaning. A king derives his power from God not because God grants him that authority, but because those he rules over see God as a meaningful thing. Within a society where God is thought to exist, and where God is a pervasive, inescapable thing of meaning, the King who claims such blessing is now backed up by an entire Order of Meaning birthed by that God. How a king is able to convince the rest of us that God has given him Divine Right is of course complicated, helped along by already-existing institutions who maintain the Order of Meaning in which that God is at the head. Also, violence helps, too.

While a traditional anarchist or Marxist (or even just an atheist) might protest that the God at the head of such an Order of Meaning is merely fictional or constructed, this doesn't actually change the power of the God. As long as enough people within a society believe that there is such a God, and that such a God also grants sovereignty to leaders, and that others (priests, diviners, etc.) can accurately determine that God's will, whether or not the God actually exists is utterly irrelevant.

This same mechanism wherein the Sacred sustains an Order of Meaning applies just as much to the Celtic and Germanic ideas of Sacred Kingship as it does to Liberal Democracy's concept of the consent-of-the-governed. Though it may have been Druids or Shamans or Priestesses declaring what the gods willed before, and though it may be elections and the media and politicians declaring what the people will now, God (or the Sacred) never disappeared as the originator of Authority.

Though many modern Polytheists, Christian Fundamentalists, or Islamic Radicals might use such a knowledge to claim that the Sacred therefore is the true source of Authority (and a source we must return to if we first acknowledge that such a Sacred exists), such a fascistic rush misses another important aspect of the space the Sacred occupies.

While I name certain experiences gods, I do not choose to therefore bow down to them, nor do they demand such a thing. I am aware of Brighid's presence and say hello, or immerse myself into the world of meaning which opens when she's around, but I don't ask her what she therefore demands of me. When something happens which I ascribe to the influence of Arianrhod, I do not kneel or vow to serve her, nor does she ask me to.

It is only certain others, those who teach things about gods–who claim to experience them and draw power from them–who demand that I do such a thing. No god has ever said, "follow me," no deity has ever asked that I give myself over to them in return for riches or power, no sacred being has ever threatened to punish me if I do not do as they say. But plenty of priests have.

Gods don't demand obedience, but humans certainly do. An employer may certainly use threats to co-erce me to do more work, a politician might certainly promise fortune if I grant him consent through ballot, a religious leader has absolutely promised great power and magic if I follow them. And in each of these cases, the demand or threat is backed up by an Order of Meaning in which such obedience is derived from a 'greater' source.

Consider: the employer has more money than I, and the hierarchy which sustains Capitalism is clear. The politician, once elected, may indeed wield the sort of power that might make me rich, but only because a political system already exists which grants the elected power over the rest of us. If I believe in the same god(s) of the religious leader and accept their claims to speak on a god's behalf, I may decide that my personal autonomy is a fair sacrifice.

That is, gods don't demand I bow to them. It is others who demand that things be bowed to, or accept an Order of Meaning where bowing to things is what you do.

Those who demand gods be served and worshiped often tell us that it is "because they are gods." This is, of course, no different from a parent saying to a child, "because I said so," or a police officer stating, "it's against the law." In all cases, the reason for the obedience comes from the supposed source of the command itself (parent, god, police). Or, put another way: Authority must be obeyed because it's Authority, and an Authority is an Authority because an Authority said so.

## The Empty Thrones

Returning to Jung's theory that a thing like a god had possessed the people of Germany, we can start to wonder why there's even a space within us to be possessed in the first place. And remembering that the Sacred has always been used by political powers to create an Order of Meaning in which their authority is secured, we need need ask why such a trick works.

The gods may exist outside ourselves, but the thrones upon which some of us put them don't. Instead, those thrones exist within. Gods inhabit the spaces we make for them in our world, just as a lover inhabits our consciousness. They become not just an outside thing, but an inside thing, taking root in our heart, our dreams, our thoughts.

Put a lover on a throne and their existence is no longer just a beautiful thing to us, but a thing of Order. Put their desires and concerns first above any other, and they no longer just co-create your meaning, they become it. You become subsumed into their existence, a servant, building your life around them rather than with them. It isn't uncommon to hear someone say of their lover, "they are the reason I exist."

It does not matter whether the lover desires such a thing at all. Most wouldn't ascend that throne, if it is to be called love. But it is not really up to them. A lover might decide I am his all regardless of whether I'd want to be such a thing (I don't), and I would then experience him as a will-less person, too eager to please, too readily disappointed when I do not fully occupy the ascended place he's made for me.

It seems it is the same with the gods. Perhaps there are some gods happy to have eager servants willing to absolve their own personality (and responsibility) into them. I do not imagine this does those gods well in the end. For instance, the racists and fascists who invoke Odin and the northern gods to justify their hatred seem to do Odin no good; he becomes, like the Christian devil, a shadow-pit into which all the blame for evil is dumped. Worse, such followers do precisely the same thing as the followers of the

# Witches In A Crumbling Empire

Christian god did, demanding conformity of belief and killing those who won't submit to their new order of meaning.

The thrones upon which we'd put a lover or a god seem to exist regardless of their desires. And that makes me wonder where such things come from: why, really, would we elevate any other being to a place of Authority besides ourselves?

The answer is probably that we've been taught to. We're taught from our youngest years to obey, to acquiesce, to comply. Our parents teach this, our elders and teachers. Police teach this, and tax collectors and jailers. Employers teach this, and journalists and bullies.

Elevate and heed the will of your parents, and you will not get punished. Hearken and obey the words of your teachers and elders, and you will not get shunned or go to detention. Fear and listen to the demands of police, and you will not get shot. Work hard, give up hours of your life and discipline yourself, and you will not get fired and go hungry.

It is our societies which carve the thrones of Authority into our souls, and there are too many others willing to sit upon them.

Putting gods upon those thrones instead of human leaders may actually seem an attempt at freedom. If Brighid occupies the highest Authority of my life, one might think I'd be less likely to obey others. But she doesn't actually fit in that seat, nor does she seem to want to sit in it. The only way for me to keep her there would be to force her into it, bind her to the armrests, chain her feet to the floor. "Stay there and be my master," I'd have to say, "tell me what to do so I am no longer responsible for my actions."

I don't think she'd take that well.

Others might claim she already sits there, that she sits on their own thrones, that she demands this. One sees this often with certain war gods like Odin or The Morrigan, but those gods aren't really much for sitting.

## No Masters

It is probably not possible to destroy the thrones. Perhaps once carved from the etheric stone of our wills, the thrones never go away. Taught from birth that someone must always have more say than others, disciplined while still crawling across the floor that some must always be lower and some must always be higher, maybe we can never unlearn this.

So perhaps it's best if we sit on those thrones ourselves. I think we usually do anyway, and merely displace our blame and guilt when we do something awful, or something does not turn out well. Afterall, we choose to obey, we choose to submit, we choose to debase our nature before the will of others.

If we sit on our own thrones, we might better resist those who'd coerce us. When others demand we obey their Authority, they'd have to topple us from our own power. When hatred points to the weak and oppressed as the cause of our own weakness, we'd be strong against such designs.

Those thrones are, after all, the very seat of our own power.

The "Wotanic spirit" that awakened into the world during the rise of Hitler is not much different from the great Authorities that have arisen in any other time. The lockstep obedience, the subservience to a greater power, the sublimation of individuality and the hatred of difference has inhabited humans many times before, and seems to arise now again.

Against such a thing, only those who know no other authority but their own might stand. But there would need to be many of us, many more than there are now. All the self-actualization in the world won't protect us from bullets or bombs, gas-chambers or prison-cells. No matter how liberated we are, without many others likewise liberated we stand alone.

Our liberation is always contingent on the liberation of others.

What would the world be like if more of us occupied our own thrones? Where freedom from coercion and the divine right of self-mastery became the primary values of our societies? As long as those with whom I interact are enchained by the will of others, I could only ever be an actualised self alone, if such a thing were even possible. To become more my self, I need others to teach me how they become their selves. To be free from the coercion of others, others around me must know what coercion even is,

And here's where the gods, temporarily unseen, resurge back like an immense tide. Beings existing outside our enchainment, needing neither to coerce nor force but merely be: are they not the very ideal of our own freedom?

That we would put them on thrones, enchain their meaning and extract it for own desire to rule everyone but ourselves—the only result of such a thing is rivers of blood running down streets or ziggurats, slaughter and manacles and camps. But if instead they are guides of our liberation, themselves unchained, themselves unmastered and unmastering, they are exactly what we might need to oppose whatever new thing is awakening in our world.

# Witches In A Crumbling Empire

We already have guides for this sort of thing. The women and men who snuck into factories under the cover of night, smashing the machinery of the rich Capitalists, claimed to follow a spectral king. "No general but Ludd," went their slogan, "did the worker any good." The Whiteboys of Ireland did the same, following a spectral land-goddess, issuing evictions in her name. Not obedience, not submission, but liberation.

Perhaps our gods, like Ludd, will agree to guide us. But we must be clear whose hands are unshackling others, whose hammers are smashing the machines, and who's actually supposed to be sitting on those thrones.

# *The World Without Forms*

*I said to a friend: we see the darkness, and some go in.*

*It is the Abyss.*

*We have to find out what is there, to find out if there is meaning. And we see only the abyss. And some go mad. And some never return. And some—*

*And some, I said, come back wielding light against that darkness. Seeing nothing, we bring back fire, we light lamps, candles, torches. We hold light that isn't ours, as how else would any else see?*

Terror often greets the far-off glances on the faces of those who return from the Abyss. The lone wanderers who walked boldly into the darkness past the boundary of fire- or street-light, the mad poet, the uncouth heretic, the unshowered witch: their reckless journeys are not celebrated when they return.

Like the ones who "walk away from Omelas," they did not know to where they were going, only somewhere not-here, not the streets full of opulent wealth and the joyous cries of liberation made possible by a founding horror. But unlike in Le Guin's story, the city is the world, and there is nowhere else to go except back to those same streets, their eyes no longer glinting with the shallow laughter of civilization but nevertheless lit with fire.

# Witches In A Crumbling Empire

It is their own fire, and it is a fire others are right to fear. It is a fire that can reforge the world.

I am what some might call an Egoist. I can also be described as a Nihilist, a mystic, an esotericist, a witch, a Pagan, an Anarchist, and also a Marxist. None of these labels actually mean anything: they are only useful when attempting to speak as the locals speak, to use the prescribed language of Capitol/Capital, treating "words that stay'" with the same fetishism which Marx ascribes to commodity-as-currency.

It is generally easier to list what I reject (for those of you checking-off boxes on mental clipboards) than it is to begin the litany of what I embrace. Few have the time: there are stories that must be told for each thing before they can be understood, and such narration seems mere obfuscation to those for whom reductionism and essentialism (as endemic to the American Left as it is to the Right) are unconscious requirements to get at the "truth."

I will tell you what I do not like. I do not like racism or racialism; I do not like gender or genderism. I do not like property or propriety, nor do I like borders and what they define. Also, Capitalism and Liberal Democracy and Empire are my least favorite things in the world, along with their shadow, Fascism.

Here, though, I should remind you: "Fascism" means nothing at all. It is a word invoked by people overcome with a strong urge to shore up the ruins of Empire by recourse to even more tenuous concepts with even less material basis: Tradition, Race, Gender, Morals, the Nation. Though the words are mere sounds we make with our throats or symbols printed with ink or displayed on screens, they each serve to outline vaguely (and by their vagueness gain more power) ideas which nevertheless have great power in the realm of the human social.

Max Stirner called these ideas "spooks." Others would call these "constructs." I prefer to name them spectres or egregores. They are also the mythic, and it's the realm of the mythic I understand best, which is also the realm the Fascists are trying to take from us.

## Spooks That Kill

Carl Jung gave a speech in 1936 in which he suggested a "Wotanic spirit" had begun to inhabit the National Socialists, as if the people had become possessed by a god:

> *Perhaps we may sum up this general phenomenon as Ergriffenheit — a state of being seized or possessed. The term postulates not only an Ergriffener (one who is seized)*

*but, also, an Ergreifer (one who seizes). Wotan is an Ergreifer of men, and, unless one wishes to deify Hitler-- which has indeed actually happened — he is really the only explanation.*

Jung invokes his theory of gods as pre- and un-conscious archetypal drives to defend his thesis, but like much of the rest of Jung's work, it's always unclear whether he believed there was not really a god there. But Jung does not quite mean what we generally think of as a god. Wotan is a "buried drive" within the Germanic people, one which essentially haunts the race until it becomes manifest.

> *"Because the behaviour of a race takes on its specific character from its underlying images, we can speak of an archetype "Wotan." As an autonomous psychic factor, Wotan produces effects in the collective life of a people and thereby reveals his own nature....It is only from time to time that individuals fall under the irresistible influence of this unconscious factor."*

Jung's racial essentialism here is tragic and prefigures the biological and genetic essentialism which now dominates Western thought. However, the concept of a mass possession by an unconscious form fits incredibly well with what we know of Nationalism.

Consider the World Trade Center attacks in 2001 in the United States. After the attacks, people experienced (and were diagnosed with) trauma from watching the explosions on television, so much so that some (including otherwise sane and clear-thinking friends of mine) for a little while believed they had either actually been present at the event or had a close friend or family member within the destroyed towers. Worse, many otherwise virulently anti-war people suddenly regained national pride, literally waving flags with such civic devotion that one would have thought their life depended upon it.

Devotion to the Nation after such traumatic events often takes on both a religious quality (similar to that of evangelical Christians) while displaying symptoms of mass hysteria. The Nation appears to haunt the actions of the individuals, manifesting and reifying itself as if by possession or seizing.

What Jung noticed regarding the possession of the German people by "Wotan" is this same process. And while one need not believe it was Wotan who possessed his people (I do not—I've asked him myself), Jung's assertion that a mythic force can operate on the psyche is hardly a unique idea. The same function was described by Max Stirner as spooks, ideological and philosophical forms which exert influence when they are unconsciously accepted as really-existing.

# Witches In A Crumbling Empire

## Spook, Spectre, Egregore

Jung's theory of archetypes, as well as Stirner's theory on spooks, may have been influenced by an occult theory regarding near-deific spirits known as egregores. An egregore (Greek for "watcher") is a spirit composed of the memories, knowledge, personality, and intentions of a group, which either arises organically from the activities and interactions of the group or is constructed willfully by the group.

Egregores could be called "group minds," though they exist autonomously (like Jung's archetypal Wotan) and maintain the cohesion, survival, and collective identity of a group beyond the individual goals of each member. Unlike an archetype, an egregore does not spring from the un-conscious/pre-conscious mind, but rather the myriad actions and interactions of those within in. Unlike a god, an egregore is not something one worships or necessarily invokes. They can be constructed, but after their construction the apparent life they take on is much more complex than what they were constructed to be.

A more accurate explanation may be to say that they are real-ised; brought from the realm of infinite possibility, the world without forms, into the more finite realm of social existence. Yet another theory is that they become inhabited after-the-fact by pre-existing spirits, similar to the way many animistic cultures build shrines as houses that benevolent spirits (or fairies, etc.) will want to move into.

Like Jung's Wotan and Stirner's spook (and to some degree Derrida's "Spectre"), the egregore describes the apparent realness of a thing despite its disconnection from the material world. There is no "there" there, and yet it functions always as if there were, manifesting itself in the actions of those who live within its realm of influence or meaning. And it thus acts also as if it were a god, making demands upon its followers who constantly (and often unconsciously) manifest its existence.

This same process has been described by other means by post-colonialist theorists. Dipesh Chakrabarty, particularly, proposes in his introduction to *Provincializing Europe* that it is precisely European exceptionalism that prevents us from seeing how those of us in Liberal Democratic societies still "inhabit these forms even as we classify ourselves as modern or secular." Similarly, Frantz Fanon and James Baldwin speak to the way that belief in whiteness and its psychological manifestations seem to inhabit those who, in Baldwin's words, "believe they are white."

One need not necessarily accept a supernatural explanation for the way the mythic manifests as-if it is real in order to comprehend this idea. Benedict Anderson's formulation of the Nation as an "imagined community" also points to the same mythic and Egregoric functioning. For him, the Nation is a modern constructed form creating an indefensible (yet fully-manifest) sense of (false) horizontal kinship with complete strangers. As Anderson says, making "it possible, over the past two centuries, for so many millions of people not so much to kill as willing die for such limited imaginings."

America exists; yet we cannot point merely to the constitution of the United States, nor to its government and institutions, soldiers and politicians and police, and say: this is America. America exists within the psyche of Americans, constantly reproduced through self-description and unconscious acceptance of its goals, desires, and inevitability. America is an egregore, a god-form, inhabiting the psyche of its individual constituents, like Jung's Wotan: "…an autonomous psychic factor, …produc[ing] effects in the collective life of a people…"

## The Fascists Know What We Prefer To Forget

Race, Gender, and all other identity categories function this same way. Gays imagine themselves part of a 'gay community,' yet there is no such thing, only an imagined kinship with people who just happen to like sex with people who have the same gender as themselves. A horrific attack on people who call themselves gay (such as the Pulse massacre in Orlando) thus manifests in individual gays elsewhere (as was the case for myself and many of my gay friends) as an attack on us as well.

We see this egregoric manifestation even stronger in whiteness. Whiteness has no material basis, yet it does not need one to manifest through the social interactions of humans. Whiteness possesses the white person, and appears to inhabit their interactions with people possessed by other egregoric racial categories (Black, etc.) regardless of their oppositional nature. In fact, the conflict and tension between egregores only further refines and entrenches their influence and power.

Neither the conservative Right nor most of the liberal or radical Left challenge these egregores. Instead, they strengthen and re-invest these egregores with power by insisting they are real and meaningful fields of social struggle (regardless of their final goals). We see this most tragically on the Left, which generally accepts the constructed nature of identities, yet also insists identity is a valid (if not foundational) field of political struggle.

# Witches In A Crumbling Empire

Consider the problem of Gender. Most Leftists accept Judith Butler's proposition that gender is performative, not essential or biological (likewise the Egoist position). Yet, particularly on the "Social Justice" Left, essentialism and a fear of straying too far from Liberal Democratic forms creates a contradictory position, seen particularly in the arguments around trans women. On the one hand, Leftists insist woman is a constructed category, yet then assert that trans women are women. That is, woman is constructed, but in order to liberate another constructed category, trans women (as category) are absolutely (essentially) part of a woman (as category), making both again essentialist, Similarly, maleness is a category that the Left generally seeks to make irrelevant, but then the Left reduces men to an essential category in which every man essentially causes exploitation, violence, and oppression ("#yesallmen").

Even if it were only the Left attempting to define the boundaries of these egregoric categories, we would find ourselves in an interminable deadlock. Unfortunately, there is a much stronger and less self-conscious current which already understands the great power these egregores have over the actions of humans.

A brief glance at the Nazi project is probably sufficient for us to grasp how Fascism not only is more comfortable with the egregoric nature of these concepts, but also understands how best to manipulate them. Nazi theorists (social, occult, legal, scientific, etc.) cobbled together a new mythic reality for Germany quite quickly. Tibetan and Hindu spirituality, Nordic and Germanic folklore, and general occult studies as well as previously oppositional and antagonist political, social, and scientific forms all became part of the egregore of Nazism, seizing the mythic imagination of a (likewise mythic) Nation.

Consider: before the Nazis, the Aryan race was a mere fringe scientific theory. During the Nazi ascension, the Aryan race was a thing, alive, "self-evident." So, too, Germany itself: suddenly a nation created only three decades before arose fully-formed with an ancient history as if it had always been there.

Did the Nazi theorists actually believe their own mythic creation? Or were they consciously creating something new? It's impossible to know. The same question could be asked of Lenin and Stalin: did they really believe in the existence of the Worker?

Or more controversially regarding the identity politics of the Left: gays did not exist as a category in the 1800's, nor did trans people. When the political category/egregoric identities of gay and trans arose, suddenly they were self-evident, alive, meaningful, and strangest of all: "true." Did those who constructed gayness and trans identity know they were making something up? How many who embrace these identities (unless they've really read Foucault) even realize that they do not stretch back into prehistory, let alone before the 20th century?

The point here is not to unravel the nightmare of Left identity politics, only to show how Leftists unconsciously do the same thing that Fascists consciously do. Leftists construct identities and egregores without any reference to the material world, yet then quickly accept them as if they have always existed, just as a Nationalist embraces the Nation and a White Supremacist embraces the White Race.

Leftism (and anti-fascism) as it currently exists is thus insufficient for combating the mythic power of Fascism until we acknowledge how much of this mythic, egregoric power we've not only ceded to Fascists, but then clumsily mimic.

## The World Without Forms

An essay by Alexander Reid Ross recently warned against the danger of "Post-Left," Egoist, mythic, and anti-civilizational thought. What these "potential intersections" with Fascism all have in common, however, is a rejection of the egregoric spooks over which the Left and Fascists are currently warring. Also, they all have at least an apparent understanding of the mechanisms by which the egregoric functions, and they each assert the freedom of the individual over these forms as a primary goal.

Ross's essay suggests that these positions seem close to the border past which all is fascist. That apparent proximity, though, is not what he suspects it to be. Rather, the extreme distance of most Leftism from the mythic (and its long complicity with Liberal Democratic secular exceptionalism) makes these non- and anti-fascist positions seem "close" to Fascism.

Leftism—especially American anti-fascism—has been so lost in the world of identities and forms that it has forgotten that they are only merely that: forms. Thus, any who reject the world of forms, or create new ones, will be seen as immediately suspect.

Were the current forms (Liberal Democracy, Capitalism, the Nation, Gender, Race, etc.) worth keeping around, then this error would not be so catastrophic. Some are certainly anti-fascist only because it threatens Liberal Democracy, and perhaps it is no longer true to say that Leftism (at least in its American iterations) is anti-imperialist or anti-capitalist any longer, regardless of how much it claims otherwise.

# Witches In A Crumbling Empire

If, however, we are anti-fascists because we are also pro-something else, something besides the current egregoric forms which lead only to exploitation, oppression, and the destruction of the earth, then we must stop looking away from the mythic power we have ceded to the Fascists.

We can see how we've done this by looking at one of the symbols that anti-fascists use to diagnose whether someone is a Fascist: the Black Sun. Though proximity doesn't prove causation, this is generally a good rule of thumb. However, little to no attention is ever given to why Fascists invoke the Black Sun.

The secret of the Black Sun is actually quite simple, and it's one that Fascists do not own. Stare at the sun in the sky and something odd happens. It appears first to turn deep red, and then goes black and starts to spin as your retina burns. It appears to go flat as it moves, revealing a deep Abyss as if all light, and all reality is merely a black hole. It also sears itself as an after-image, lingers there for hours (if not days), and creates the perception that there is actually nothing behind the sun.

I do not suggest every white boy and girl who puts an image of the Black Sun as their iPhone background has experienced the same mystical transformation that medieval alchemists name *nigredo*, nor do I assert that it is an Abyssal truth limited to mystical traditions or European-derived thought (the Sufis and many animist traditions describe a similar experience). Still, it should intrigue us that in at least one Fascist strain, a rite exists which inducts the initiate into the nihilist/spiritual world without forms.

From that world, through such an initiation, it is easy to transcend societal restraints and enter into the pre-formal realm of perception. Outside the constraints of socially-constructed identity and morality, any new thought is possible and any new form is acceptable specifically because "possible" and "acceptable" no longer apply. More so, the experience strengthens the will of the initiate: the vision was survived, the mind intact.

Those who've studied and felt the inebriating mix of mythic power and indomitable will evinced by Jack Donovan and the Wolves of Vinland will understand my meaning here. Donovan has been able to create an intoxicating, egregoric, mythic conception of the world, cobbling together fragments of the past with terrifyingly violent new ideologies which are pristine in their coherence. There is raw, seductive, violent power here that functions on the primal (pre-conscious, libidinal) level against which anti-fascists have no other defense except no-platforming.

## Reclaiming What We've Thrown Away

If I here seem full of praise for something so horrifying, it is not because I am, but because you may have become so separated from your own mythic power that you've forgotten you can do this too, towards a more affirming and fair world rather one of hierarchy and hatred.

I suspect we shun this power for two reasons. First, anyone returning from the Abyss with such mythic visions, transcending the egregores by which the rest of us are ruled, will always be initially marked as a heretic or an outcast. Only when we find others who have seen the same things or who find meaning in these new dreams can such mystics find acceptance. The other reason? We've so long ago ceded to others our power to make the world that we are more happy to leave such delvings to the Fascists than realize we are complicit in our own enchainment.

The world without forms, where we can again reclaim our power, is what Stirner and the Egoists embrace. It is also what Bataille sought, as did his close friend, the Jewish mystic Walter Benjamin. From that world we see both the infinite possibility of human liberation and the infinite delusions under which we have for too long struggled. It is also where we can learn how to be Walter Benjamin's "real state of emergency" which will eventually make Fascism untenable.

The Nation is a false thing that only has power because we give it power. Gender, race, class, religion, morals—even the self itself—are all constructs. Civilization is a spook, one to which we are always subject because we believe there is such a thing as civilization, because other people believe there is such a thing as civilization, and because all of us fail to remember that civilization is just an idea in our heads that causes us to cohere around it and give it more power. Thus, the Fascist who warns that civilization is under threat from Islam, or trans people, or Cultural Marxism—as well as the Liberal-Leftist who warns that civilization is under threat from Fascism—are both still merely fighting for control over the egregore of Civilization.

Any anti-fascism which seeks to break not only the power of the Fascists but also the power of the forms the Fascists wish to control must refuse to accept the forms themselves. Race, Gender, the Nation, Civilization–these are not our forms, they are forms which enchain us, they do not exist in the world we wish to build, and we must stop pretending otherwise. Instead, we must make new forms while always conscious that they are only just forms, forms we can change at will because it is our will which births them.

We must also refuse to cede the mythic—and the embrace of the self—to the Fascists. The "post-leftists" and the Egoists and those who've read Bataille, and also those who've read Baldwin or Fanon or Chakrabarty, and especially all those who would dare walk past the forest's edge in darkness and find there new truths, regardless the consequences—it is to them where we must look for the rituals which will free us all. It is them, and nothing else, who can finally exorcise Fascism's spectre from our world.

# *Good White Men*

Once sitting in a cafe on lunch break from my former job as a social worker for homeless people a man told me this:

"The only good white men are the ones who know they should be shot in the face because all they are capable of is harm."

I kept sipping my coffee, watching the veins in his neck bulge like thick cable. His non-binary queer white friend shot me a disgusted look and handed me back the zine I'd given them both. Then, to her shaking friend she offered soothing words, stroking the masculinity he pretended he hadn't just wielded, calming him with the emotional labor skills drilled into her assigned-female body by the same cis-het white patriarchy they both claimed to fight.

I watched them leave together three years ago. I watch them leave together now in my head, wondering whatever happened to that man.

We'd been discussing revolution. They were both dour youths, certain in their short lives they knew the divinely-encoded fate of humanity, the impossibility of change, and the self-evident truths about the nature of peoples and their behaviors. Patriarchy was hard-coded into the cocks of men, domination genetically-woven into the bones and breath of whites, and all that was left was for a few elect to hide in forests while the rest of the world collapsed.

# Witches In A Crumbling Empire

"Why so dire?" I'd asked, suggesting organizing enough folks together might prove to be a better idea.

It was then I was told the only path to being a "good white man."

There was so much I'd wanted to ask him about. Still is. But I'll most likely never get that chance, and am left with only speculation and curiosity. Though it isn't of course the only time I've ever heard words like that. You have too, I'm sure. People born with light-skinned penises are privileged murdering/raping machines, guilty by birth of the most horrific of crimes and inescapably predestined to enact them at every turn. By degrees such a person might mollify some of those sins, but never quite expiate them. A lifetime of dismantling privilege or a full switch of gender might possibly suffice to grant passage through the pearly gates of social justice, but even those acts are hardly guarantees.

Like the Methodism of John Wesley so popular with industrialists in England, the path to perfection in such reckonings is prescriptively Sisiphysian. The boulder will never rest at the top, it will always topple back down, and the point is anyway to always be treading the mill, accepting such a fate just as the worker needed accept their treading to the mills each morning. Back home at night, sleep, awake and do more penance before an ever-wrathful god who doles out just enough scratch to keep you alive so you can return.

How it came to be as such confounds. Could those who first iterated a politics of liberation through the framework of woman-ness and Black-ness have predicted they'd merely repeated Calvinism? That in their glorious rebellions they'd merely replicated the slave-morality taught to them by their ancestor's masters? We cannot know, and the more useful questions arise elsewhere, amongst which the most urgent–and the one finally I hear people asking again–is this:

"who does this really serve?"

I think that is why I am thinking about that man again, so certain the shape of my genitals and the tone of my skin made me a racist and rapist. We'd not been talking about my cock at all, or about race, but about the possibility of revolution. His (and his friend's) certainty that there existed an entire genre of humanity reduced only to base barbaric instincts (an unmistakable repetition of the very same things said about Black men) assured them that any relational politics, any organization against the powerful, was impossible. There would be no revolution because of white penises, and so it's best if we all hide in the woods to escape from them.

This same trope repeats in every other iteration of individualistic identit-arianism. There will be no revolution because white women, or cis people, or abled-people, or heterosexuals, or binary people. They are all in the way, stopping an ever-dwindling elect from achieving our liberation against systems and hierarchies and structures that cannot be seen and thus cannot actually be fought.

Unlike these occulted enemies, however, the people destroying the environment have names and addresses. So, too, the owners of factories and oil companies, the politicians and police who defend them, the heads of media empires that pump out endless falsehoods between advertisements, the heads of banks and arms manufacturers, generals and presidents and mayors. They are not just systems and structures: they are flesh and blood, and they are actually killing people. Many of them have penises, and many of those penises (I assume probably) are white-skinned. Like Nazis looking for Jewishness by checking the foreskins of prisoners, the identitarians of both fascist and social justice strands divine from pale skin and penises the indelible mark of the power to dominate.

So, as the once-strong movements of social justice dwindle into ever more isolated cadres of intersectional elect, their fascist shadow looms ever larger, equally obsessed with the white phallus. Yet fixation on genitalia and skin-tone are not their only shared trait, for they both cling deeply to what their masters taught their ancestors. Do not work with those not like you. Blame your suffering on symbols and skin. Purify yourself to be made holy and worthy in the eyes of your lords, who wield over you the power of life and death as they collect your rent and dole out your wages.

As that fascist shadow looms larger, claiming more and more people told by social justice activists that their skin color and cocks make them innately, irrevocably evil, I doubt there will be many places for that man and his friend to run.

Perhaps they will still find some utopia in the woods, far from society and its horrors.But I fear for them that such peace will be as elusive as finding "good white men" who will shoot themselves in the face for being born with pale skin and a penis.

# *Barbarians in the Age of Mechanical Reproduction*

*The old world is dying, the new world struggles to be born. Here in the interregnum arises morbid systems.*

–Antonio Gramsci

*Increasingly, people are restless. The engineers group themselves into competing teams, but neither side seems to know what to do, and neither seems much different from the other. Around the world, discontent can be heard. The extremists are grinding their knives and moving in as the machine's coughing and stuttering exposes the inadequacies of the political oligarchies who claimed to have everything in hand. Old gods are rearing their heads, and old answers: revolution, war, ethnic strife. Politics as we have known it totters, like the machine it was built to sustain. In its place could easily arise something more elemental, with a dark heart.*

–The Dark Mountain Manifesto

## The Wolf Trap

In what is now Germany, particularly in the area called Lower Saxony, a certain symbol appeared etched on stones and trees, demarcating forests left wild for hunting. In such old forests, the wolf, that heavily-culled European apex predator, still ran free, threatened only by ritualized royal chases in which an iron hook was used to trap them. The shape of the trap inspired those border symbols, symbols which also bore its name: wolfsangel (wolf-hook).

Centuries later, peasants angry at the increasingly authoritarian rule of princes and their refusal to honor ancient land-use customs revolted, wielding the symbol as their banner. Then, in the early part of the 20th century, its most well-known use began, this time not as as symbol of revolt but of authority and Empire itself. Inspired by its use in the 1910 German novel *Der Wehrwolf*, the Nazi Party and many military regiments adopted it as part of their iconography, which is how most of us know of it now.

The wolfsangel (also the Elder Futhork rune *Eihwaz*) perhaps best explains the struggle for mythic and ideological territory that has defined many of the conflicts between political forces since the birth of Liberal Democracy. Symbols, myths, and ideas seem to change hands, disappear from one place and reappear in another. Old gods and politics are re-tooled for new, darker uses, then again stolen back. The swastika appears on the feet of the Buddha, also the flag of the Nazis; Gramsci's formulation of metapolitical change becomes abandoned by European leftists and picked up by the European New Right.

In a essay at *Gods&Radicals*, Peter Gaffney examined this process through Foucault's reading of Nietzsche:

> *"This is how Foucault understands Nietzsche's concept of Entstehung, which he translates as l'émergence – or alternately as les points de surgissement (the moments, stages or positions of arising)–, by which a discourse always appears anew in the hands of historically contingent forces: "Rules are empty in themselves, violent and unfinalized; they are impersonal and can be bent to any purpose. The successes of history belong to those who are capable of seizing the rules, to replace those who had used them, to disguise themselves so as to pervert them, invert their meaning, and redirect them against those who had initially imposed them; controlling this complex mechanism, they will make it function so as to overcome the rulers through their own rules."*

There is a simpler and more raw way to envision this process, that of wars over land or sacred territory. Pope Boniface advised his priests to build their churches upon ancient pagan sites; old sacred wells where people prayed to Pagan goddesses in Europe are now all dedicated to Catholic saints or the Virgin. The sites remain, the power means something beyond the colonization and struggle. The poor and faithful still visit the sites of Druid mountains and Pagan temples, still utter prayers, but the words are different, serving different sacred orders.

It matters who holds that territory, and the wars of occupation and reclamation are fiercest at times when Empire loses its grip. Each of the three

# Witches In A Crumbling Empire

Fascist uprisings in Europe occurred at times when Liberal Democracy began to crumble, the "interregnum" in which Gramsci warned "monsters" (or morbid systems) awoke.

We are in a similar period.

In each previous instance, Communists and Anarchists relentlessly ceded mythic territory to the nationalist forces. Fascists have always better understood the relationship of power and aesthetic, because they have no qualms about using them. Leftists still fail to heed Gramsci's analysis, and rather than employ their own mythic imaginings to awaken a new world against the dying of the old, they choose now (as they did last century) to side with the Empire, that "Liberal center," which in all three instances proved not only to be poor allies, but eager assassins when the fascist threat finally manifested.

Liberal Democracy is failing again. Capitalism has entered another crisis stage, desperately seeking new resources to extract from ever-dwindling wells. The altars of Progress and Modernity demand offerings, and the priests who tend them are sharpening blades, ready to begin new sacrifices.

*Eilhwaz*, the wolfsangel, is a powerful symbol. It symbolizes Yew, the graveyard tree, the acceptance of death's inevitability that leads to heroic acts of reckless courage. As a boundary marker it warned those outside the wild that past its etched symbol roamed death, while granting permission to all those on the other side of it to use violence against what passed from its boundary into the settled lands.

From experience, I also know it to be a most powerful warding rune. It trips up those who stalk your secret meetings, protects from surprise, guards territory, and acts exactly as its name suggests: hooking wolves into a struggle to the death. No counter-magic have others found against my uses of it.

The wolfsangel was first shown to me in a vision, the last in a series of four glyphs I learned to use during ancestral work. I have used it since, even after I learned a year later that it was symbol co-opted by the Nazis. While the antifascist left has generally shown themselves quite willing to cede territory in order to keep their Liberal allies, I have no intention to, anymore than I will give up the use of the wolfsangel.

That stubborness, that refusal to give up what is mine, what is ours by right of ideological and revolutionary ancestors (of blood or otherwise), is the guiding strategy of this essay. It is also the only way to neuter a threat which exists only by our permission.

## Empires Crumbling

On the 18th of February, 2017, several hundred people gathered to hear a man speak, one who's dedicated years to studying unpopular European philosophers, seeking knowledge from gods of death and war, and cobbling together an analysis of Modernity's failings and what might be built from its ruins.

Actually, two men spoke on that subject that day, to two different crowds on two different parts of the planet. Both speakers were 'gay' men, though reject that identity in favor of self-determination. Both shape their politics of the world around an aesthetic of wild forest, unrestrained humanity, and a refusal to accept Liberal Democracy's pretensions of peace and progress.

The first man (whose name I will withhold for a short time) presented an hour-long speech on the west coast of the United States. The other presented a 20-minute talk called "Violence is Golden" in a beer hall to a group of European Identitarians at the *Institut für Staatspolitik*. His name was Jack Donovan.

By now you have probably heard his name. You will read (and I will write) it much more than I or you prefer. So be it, though—to look away is to hide from something we ourselves have birthed and empowered, and something only we can stop. I will not repeat the clumsy, panicked mistakes in the various recent exposés running through your news feed. The Southern Poverty Law Center's piece in March of 2018 was deeply flawed, Slate's essay a few months after was even more a failure. These two articles, as well as many other criticisms, have failed completely to explain his appeal while simultaneously missing the core threat of his ideas.

These and many other failures betray a deep and intentional blindness particularly within American anti-fascist and Leftist thought, the product both of a marriage to Liberal Democratic hegemony and an almost ecstatic abdication of revolutionary territory. One cannot accurately criticize Jack Donovan without also criticizing the anti-fascist Left who has taken upon themselves the task of (ineptly) opposing him. Likewise, one cannot speak about the dangers the Wolves of Vinland (and Paul Waggener's Operation Werewolf) without also telling long-stifled truths about modern society and the various Pagan, Environmental, and Anarchist movements which the Wolves of Vinland are currently poised to supplant.

This is not a comfortable task, and it is ironic that there is more risk to me in this essay than to its intended targets. That risk is not from the Wolves of Vinland's brutalist-sculpted warriors or their aesthetic of violence. I do not fear the muscles and fight-training of Waggener or Donovan (come at me, bro). Rather, it is from the established orthodoxy of American anti-fascism and its slavish worship of Liberal Democratic conceits that the vast majority of criticism for this work will likely come.

Already my admission that I am intimately acquainted with the wolfsangel has put me at risk of being considered a crypto-fascist, because many antifascist theorists police their borders not with an eye towards reclaiming lost territory, but with a terror of what lurks beyond the well-lit street lights in the dark forests into which the light of cities can never reach.

Despite the risk, I need to write this essay. Not just because I foresee further territory being abandoned as the American Left cuts out its insurrectionary heart and offers it on the altars of progress, praying that the Empire can be saved. Nor do I write this only because the future Jack Donovan and the Wolves of Vinland crave is one I do not want to see in this world. More than anything, I write this essay because, on the same day that Jack Donovan helped provide the intellectual justification for violence to a strengthening European Identitarian movement, I did the same thing for a growing Pagan anti-capitalist movement. I was the other speaker that day, 6000 miles away.

Since noting the dark poetry of such simultaneity, I've given extensive time to reading Donovan's work and regretting that our similarities did not end there. It's precisely these similarities, however, which both demand that I write this essay while also making such an essay dangerous. We occupy similar territory, outside the urbs of Liberal Democratic Empire where barbarians and wolves dwell, past the boundary markers where the reach of the *civitas* and the *polis* is declawed. I know this land, these gods, and these ideas. And I will not give them up.

## Anti-modernism in the Age of Mechanical Reproduction

*The logical result of Fascism is the introduction of aesthetics into political life. The violation of the masses, whom Fascism, with its Führer cult, forces to their knees, has its counterpart in the violation of an apparatus which is pressed into the production of ritual values.*

*--Walter Benjamin, "The Work of Art In The Age of Mechanical Reproduction."*

*"In the absence of an equally compelling counter-narrative, a significant portion of the masses will also embrace fascism, and history will be left to repeat itself."*

*--Alley Valkyrie, Propaganda in the Age of Fascism*

No discussion of Jack Donovan, the Wolves of Vinland, or Operation Werewolf can truly begin without focusing on their aesthetic. Many have tried, reducing their images to caricature, missing their sublime and intox-icating coherence, dismissing it all as if image had no power. We shall not make the same mistake.

A few minutes perusing Jack Donovan's Instagram feed is more than sufficient to reveal their aesthetic power. What Donovan wants you to see is that the Modern world is too new, too garish, that there is no place within it for people like him nor for people like you. Viewing his photos, one ima-gines he hates the imposed efficiency of florescent lights, prefers the slant of sunlight at the end of day, would use lanterns if his eyesight were better, and is allergic to gaudy colors. His is not the aesthetic of a consumer. The exact polar opposite of his proposed milieu is a Walmart, bright lights glaring off the cellophane-wrapped chemically-colored products which define most American lives. Instead, behind him are unfinished concrete walls in gyms or forests, the decayed urban or the feral wild, an old-world feel clipping out the $6 latte area of Portland, Oregon where he until recently lived.

Aesthetic is narrative. Aesthetic tells a story, and Jack Donovan's story is of anti-modernism. It is not just because he is anti-modern, but he also senses what his increasing fan-base knows and most anti-fascists refuse to admit: the modern is fucking awful. The modern is alienating, full of empty images and promises after which we all chase. Progress brings us a new iPhone each year and more flavors of Doritos, jobs in front of screens and new identities to try on and less and less land in which to play tribe with your friends.

The paradox, of course, is that it is precisely because of the modern that we experience his anti-modern vision, the same convoluted trap in which any critic of Liberal Democratic empire finds themselves. As Walter Ben-jamin noted, we are never in relationship to the subject of an image, but rather in relationship with a lens and a screen. We only ever interface with the production of images, the machinery of mass-aesthetic.

Donovan's aesthetic attempts to escape this, but it cannot. What Donovan portrays is crafted just as any other selfie is, posed, selected, filtered and cropped, uploaded into The Feed for us all to see. It is an anti-modern aesthetic made possible only by the modern, a resistance to Em-pire generated by Empire like Orwell's Emmanuel Goldstein waiting with Big Brother's pre-scripted revolt. In this way, though, he is no different from any of us. The Antifa selfie, the anti-capitalist meme: we do the same.

This paradox in which we are all trapped is not limited to the mere re-production of the anti-modern by modern means. It is an oppositional aesthetic, crafted constantly in response to the modern. What is anti-modern is determined by the modern itself, just as what is anti-oppressive within social justice is determined by the oppressive, what is Left is determined by what is Right. Audre Lourde's statement that "the master's tools can never dismantle the master's house," while originally an attack on the bourgeois goals of white feminists, just as easily describes the perpetual paradox of all resistance to the Modern.

## A Body Politic

Key to understanding Donovan's aesthetic, then, is that he is merely re-tooling the master's narrative, determined not by some mastery of the will but an almost adolescent act of opposition. Inverting Lourde's point, Donovan attempts to look like the master himself, becoming what his chosen enemies fear him to be.

Towards this end, his physique is his primary weapon, one that can command erotic respect from fully hetero-men as well as gays. He wants–needs–you to think he is hot, and even his feminist critics often write slobberingly about his body even as they then attack it. This is his success: the masculinity he wears is bold, brazen, unapologetic: it draws the sort of followers he desires while offending those socialized to find such displays of virility indicative of "toxic masculinity."

This aesthetic politics of the body is part of the core ideology not just of Jack Donovan but also of Operation Werewolf, a site run and founded by Paul Waggener. To understand its appeal, the imagery of its manifesto must be approached the same way the visual aesthetic must be: fully felt, with an eye on the backgrounds and filters:

> *Operatives can be found in countries across the world, dripping sweat on the floor of their spartan-style garage weight room, leaving blood on the dirt in the backyard boxing ring, or bringing their feral competitive style to powerlifting meets, MMA events, bars, back alleys and the savage streets of crumbling cities. They are not products of their environment- instead they change the landscape and environment around them, forgers of destiny, architects of their own becoming. They make the flesh strong, knowing that it is the only fit conveyance for a strong mind and an iron will- theirs is a mindset that accepts no weakness.*

> *Some are solitary practitioners, performing the rituals of life and death amongst the ruins of modern civilization, lone wolves howling songs of destruction and new growth in the woods that encroach on the edges of the rotting Empire, waiting for the fall. Others have made it their mission to seek each other out, forming militaristic divisions, chapters led by their strongest member, creating a war-band that seeks to carve its own myth, to create its own saga of power and might- men and women challenging each other to strive ever higher.*

Like this manifesto (powerful, until you realize it's a sloppy pastiche of Dark Mountain's manifesto and Peter Grey's *Rewilding Witchcraft*), the articles on Operation Werewolf exort the reader towards a vision of self-fulfillment on the "edges of the rotting Empire, waiting for the fall." Again, sweaty gym-forged bodies with wild forest and concrete as backdrop, perfectly selected sepia filters assuring you they aren't currently huddled over screens masturbating to porn.

Readers for whom the notion of sweat, brawls, and "accepting no weakness" is off-putting should be reminded that it is supposed to repulse you. It is not to you whom they are writing, any more than it is to the civilized urban feminist that Jack Donovan bares his torso. Resist, however, the inclination to dismiss this as negative: while Operation Werewolf is not the body-positivity of urban Social Justice, it is nevertheless the positivity of a body stretched, strained, and repeatedly broken to test its limits and "forge the will."

Here, many critics fall back upon accusations of ableism or fat-shaming. Without doubt there is no place inscribed into their aesthetic for the overweight person, nor for the chronically-ill, yet such critiques (however true within the framework of liberal Social Justice politics) fall utterly flat. They are not attempting to build an inclusive ideology, but rather one of difference and exclusion. Dismissing them on these grounds, however morally-satisfying, is utterly useless.

Anti-fascist responses to such rhetoric through the Social Justice framework not only fail, but expose an ignored and suppressed difference in their own ranks, best seen within the difference between Liberal and Leftist feminism. The former, which is the predominate form within Social Justice, argues that patriarchal violence is the primary cause of bodily oppression. On the other hand, Leftist iterations (Marxist, post-colonialist) locate the cause of such oppression (anti-disabled, anti-fat, etc.) in the Capitalist's need to turn humans into workers and the State's need to turn humans into subjects.

From a Liberal feminist ("bourgeois" or "white" feminist) view, any politics or ideology which does not treat all bodies as equal is patriarchal, and each oppression (ableism, transphobia, etc.) is an additional variant of patriarchal rule (consider Liberal feminist statements such as "homophobia is rooted in hatred of women"). To undermine the patriarchy and achieve equality within that framework, all bodies must be accorded the same worth and access, since every exclusion is a reproduction of patriarchal oppression.

# Witches In A Crumbling Empire

Marxist and post-colonial feminist frameworks dismiss such utopianism in favor of the abolition of the conditions which equates the worth of bodies to what can be derived from them: that is, Capitalism. A disabled or chronically-ill person is "worth less" (paid less) under capitalism because they can produce less for their bosses (who are usually men, but often also women). They are valued less because their labor cannot be exploited as easily.

To a Liberal feminist, patriarchy is the problem and the problems of capitalism derive from the patriarchy, not from capitalism itself. Within the feminism of Marxists and post-colonialists, Patriarchy is merely the functional aesthetic of the oppression of bodies, while capitalist control of the body is the core problem.

What Operation Werewolf advocates does not directly conflict this latter, insurrectionist feminism. If anything, people of any gender hoping to be physically strong enough to fight the inevitable police and military backlash against revolutionary actions could benefit from such exhortations. If you want to learn to fight cops or fascists, you'll need first to learn how to fight.

Too often, though, discussions regarding expanding the capacity of the body are dismissed, labeled "ableist" or "fat-shaming," and even potentially fascist. A particularly poignant example of this is the reaction to a 2016 essay from Peter Grey, a writer and publisher who has repeatedly held the line against fascist incursions into esotericism, including pulling his work from use in publications wherein fascist writers appear. Within Pagan, witch, radical, and esoteric communities, his essay *"Forging the Body of the Witch"* was held up by some as proof that the (very not-fascist) writer was potentially fascist, or at the very least engaging in ableism and fat-shaming. Another case in point: Silvia Federici's essay, *"In Praise of the Dancing Body,"* was similarly attacked as ableist because she advocates dancing as a form of bodily resistance and suggests that Capitalism has alienated us from our bodies through extensive medicalization.

Anti-civilizationist, autonomous Marxist, anarchist, and other radical writers have similarly come under such friendly-fire attacks so that, as of now, the only people actually putting forward a framework in which the potential capabilities of the body are fully-embraced are men like Jack Donovan and Paul Waggener.

This is the first example of how Leftists have ceded territory in which fascists can thrive. Leftists abandoned a political framework which embraces the body–both in its weaknesses as well as its strengths–in favor of one which disfavors (and even attacks) any celebration of human capacity as inherently oppressive. In such a world, the muscular bodies of a factory, farm, or construction worker—the very people whom Leftists once saw as a revolutionary force—are to be hidden, minimized, or even derided, lest those who do not have such bodies or cannot get them feel excluded from insurrectionist discourse.

This is why anti-fascist criticisms of Donovan (etc.) fall flat. There is nothing inherently fascist about the body work he and Operation Werewolf advocate: indeed, it is also something embraced by many suppressed forms of feminism as well. It is only territory they occupy, colonized by a fascist aesthetic. Such territory once belonged to the Left, who have become all too long happy to abandon it. Doing so means that fascists are then allowed to run free through it and claim it as their own.

## Ad Hominem

Many essays attacking Jack Donovan particularly center their critique on his aesthetic masculinity, effectively reducing his threat to his maleness. While a Slate piece devotes extensive time to his aesthetic of virility, even to the point of slobbering affection ("A beautifully muscular man of 42 who has perfected a masculine scowl…he functions as beefcake for the neofascist cause,") the Southern Poverty Law Center's essay reduces his entire appeal to that of his overt maleness, inscribing him into Alex Di Branco's thesis that it is misogyny itself which is animating new fascist movements.

Both make precisely the same mistake and only strengthen the allure of his raw, uncivilized male aesthetic. For a constructed masculine aesthetic to be a political aesthetic, it must have a nemesis. Fortunately for him, his critics easily supply that role, reducing him to his masculinity in precisely the same way they accuse men of doing to women. For most of his critics, Donovan is a meat-head, a thug, a dumb man who probably doesn't use deodorant. Such reductions reproduce the same patriarchal modes of dismissal: a woman is just her tits, Donovan is just his muscles.

Like an Antifa protester lobbing a tear gas canister back at the police, Donovan is able swiftly to redeploy these reductions to expand his audience. To understand how, consider the sort of people to whom he appeals: men like him, displaced, uncomfortable in the world, first unsure of and then later angry about the absurd rules of civilization, unable to find meaning except by escape into romantic notions of heroism and courage now that the jobs are all gone overseas. To such men, seeking something mythic, something to make them feel like they have a place in the world, ridicule of their masculinity only further entrenches their sense of alienation. When a critic ridicules his, Donovan need only hold up their insult before his audience, and suddenly his male tribalism doesn't even need a sales pitch.

Further, Jack Donovan's deep intelligence is easily missed by critics who are tricked by his aesthetic. On Instagram he stands shirtless, inked, holding a chainsaw; elsewhere he is wearing hunting gear, or grunting in a gym, drilling wood, wearing a baseball cap. He looks rural, the sort of working-class man urban liberals dismiss immediately as smelly, uneducated, and crass. Here Donovan is able to leverage an inherent prejudice within what passes for the Left in America: its anti-rural, anti-working class sentiment.

Donovan presents as the sort of man who drives large trucks, thinks forests should be clear-cut, drinks Budweiser in front of football games, and would bash the head in of a man at a rest stop who stared at his crotch. As such, he becomes too easily dismissed, his arguments reduced to mere grunts in, as the SPLC article put it, the "chorus of moaning that emanates from the Manosphere."

Donovan is no doubt aware of this, and wields these prejudices deftly against his critics. It is a trick I know well myself: I am a 6 foot 1 inch, gruff-voiced, 'masculine-presenting' man who talks more like a "bro" than a theorist. The disconnect between my appearance and my intelligence often puts critics and fans alike off-guard. Thus when my critics attempt to reduce my arguments to my male appearance, they will often appear shallow or uninformed in public forums. This same mechanism works in Jack Donovan's favor.

More so, by targeting his masculine presentation, critics also re-inforce Liberal urban elitism and undermine any other critique they offer. To reduce Donovan to his maleness is to reduce him to his perceived identity, alienating those who see misandry as unhelpful (or even dangerous) as well as lower-class men for whom muscles, power-tools, and backyard construction projects are inherent parts of daily life and work, rather than cultivated threats against women.

This is another territory ceded by the Left. The bodies (and the accompanying concerns of the body) of poor and working-class men (unless their maleness can also be shown to intersect with at least one other oppression identity) are all but completely dismissed in American Leftist discourse. It should not surprise us, then, that the aesthetic of overt, unapologetic masculinity which Donovan, Waggener, and the Wolves of Vinland celebrate would appeal to those ignored men. For such men, the aesthetic of brute maleness accompanied by deep thought and independent will shall always be more appealing than what Liberalism has to offer. Marxists and Anarchists once offered them something too, but if they still do, it cannot be found in current American antifascist discourse.

## Squatter's Rights

To see how well Donovan reclaims Leftist territory for his own, consider Donovan's book on male desire, *Androphilia*. Written in 2006, it advances a vision of homosexuality not as a genetically-deterministic identity class, but of a variation or subset of male desire. The consequences of such a view are that male-male desire is a manifestation of human choice, rather than the current Liberal dogma that gays are "born this way."

Within the vast majority of gay-rights organizing, the insistence that homosexuality is determined by biology rather than being a choice has become divine law. This ironically leaves only anti-homosexual Christian Evangelicals asserting that gay men actually have any agency in their sexual desire (by insisting it can and should be changed.)

The historical reason why it became Liberal consensus that homosexuality is an innate, essential, and biologically-determined identity has nothing to do with science. As in most cases, scientific theory follows political will, and this position was politically strategic. In order to counter the moral arguments against homosexual sex, gay-rights activists presented homosexual desire as an immutable, scientifically-determined way of being. In such a framework, since gays had no choice but to engage in homosexual behavior, moral or legal arguments that demanded they change their behavior made no sense.

This strategy certainly helped gays gain legal status within most Liberal Democracies, but it also stole from gays belief in their agency. Thus, I as a man who desires men actually have no say in the matter, because my genes make me desire men. The "Leftist" position now, at least the Social Justice position, depoliticizes will and individual choice, adopting the very same Nazi logic which located social-identity (Homosexual, Jew) in the body and then destroyed the body to destroy the identity.

Donovan's arguments in *Androphilia* cunningly leverage this transposition. Arguing that male homosexual desire is just another configuration of male desire is really the more liberatory position. Even more (unfortunately) to his credit, rather than arguing to heterosexual men that they should accept male-male desire on account of Liberal Democratic rights, he argues that heterosexual men should embrace their already-existent desire for males.

The territory here that Donovan is able to claim—and the primary reason his ideas have so much resonance—is precisely what was ceded by Leftists who hitched their liberatory politics to the dreams of Liberal Democratic progress. While no doubt forged from a sense of pragmatic urgency (homosexuals were—and are—killed at rather high rates), the political subjectivity and loss of agency such a politics created cannot be easily undone.

Attempts to offer another narrative are often virulently attacked. I have never felt I was "born this way," yet to write openly about this is to elicit some rather intense rage from Social Justice activists who see such a position as a sign of my "heteronormative privilege,"" that I am not "queer enough" to speak on such matters, or that I must have "internalized homophobia." In a situation where the leftist position insists sexual selection is innate and pre-determined, it should not surprise anyone that, as according to the Slate article, gays are being attracted to fascism. But contrary to the conclusion of the author, Donovan's position offers homosexuals back the agency that Liberal Democracy stripped from them in return for protections. This is not due to anything revolutionary or even original in Donovan's thinking, but the same abdication of territory (in this case, an abdication of will) that leftists have elsewhere enacted.

## Masculinity as Simulacrum

Returning to the matter of Donovan's particular aesthetic: Donovan presents a vision of a man who is fully in touch with his will, comfortable with his desire for other men, unapologetic about his body, and unconcerned with what anyone thinks of him. In his books we see this aesthetic turn into an entire ethic, a religious redemption of the masculinity which bourgeois feminism sees as the primary cause of oppression.

Here we can re-introduce crucial discussion regarding Donovan's misogyny, and also see how all these abandoned Leftist positions re-animate into something quite morbid. Donovan loathes women. *Androphilia* blames almost every horrible thing on women; gay men shop because of women, gay men kill themselves because they are trying to be like women, trans women are men who have internalized everything that feminists told them about themselves.

His later books, *The Way of Men* and *Becoming a Barbarian*, both repeat this same ressentiment. Men are soft because of women, men stay at home instead of adventure because of them. Men don't have enough men-only spaces because women expect to be everywhere, etc.. It all starts to sound so absurd that it's easy to miss that he is parodying the excesses of bourgeois feminism in reverse. In fact, his entire construct of hypermasculine existence could have been constructed by bourgeois feminism itself. If there is anything truly tragic about Jack Donovan's vision of maleness—the one which fills the pages of his books and his Instagram feed–it is that it was created by the very same feminism which he so deeply loathes.

Such a reality, however, does not reduce its power. Jean Baudrillard expanded Walter Benjamin's work on aesthetics by noting how, now that we only have reproduction of art, we now also only have reproduction of politics. The Real we imagine is always a copy, a simulation of the real. Those copies and simulations become how we determine what is real, affecting our behaviour and the construction of our identities. Whereas once the aesthetic was the visual representation of a way of being, the aesthetic is now our only blueprint. We do not know what it is like to be masculine except by the representation of the masculine, anymore than we know what it is to be anti-modern without representations of the anti-modern.

More dangerous, however, is that the negatives of images reproduce themselves as well. The aesthetic of hyper-masculinity from which Donovan and Waggener build their politics is produced from the negative space of Liberal feminist critiques which reduce men to enemy, alpha-oppressor, toxic, and dangerous. But negative space is never truly empty, just as territory no longer claimed is never truly vacant. We should be hardly surprised, then, that Wolves have moved into the places we have abandoned, inhabiting ideological homes which were once ours.

It is not clear, however, that many have the strength or will to kick them out.

# *Witches in a Crumbling Empire*

Witchcraft is political.

By political we do not mean it is aligned with certain electoral parties or statist tendencies. There is nothing inherently Liberal or Conservative, Democratic or Republican, to our magic and practices.

Witchcraft is political because witches are political subjects. We live in cities and towns and nations which make laws to which we are subjected. Our access to the world around us is limited by political structures, not least of which is the capitalist notion of private property.

I cannot merely go outside my door and build a small shrine to a cross-roads deity in the middle of an intersection; the land under that crossroads is not mine to work with, at least according to the laws of this city. Further, it's sealed over by asphalt and constantly traversed by large machines called cars that might kill me if I were to stand in the middle of it.

There is a relevant law in the United States, under which I've been previously arrested. *Pedestrian Interference of Traffic*, it's called, and in many places it can land you a year in prison for daring to interrupt the all-important movement of sport utility vehicles from office to suburban home. No better law describes the upside-down world of modern Capitalism and the status of witch as political subject better than this law. People who travel with their feet can become criminals if they dare stand in the way of people traveling in machines.

The very human act of walking upon two feet is fantastic. It's a complex movement of balance, one few other species have ever done. Yet we need almost nothing to do it, just the same sort of things we need to do anything else with our muscles and bones. We need food to turn into energy, air to fill our blood with oxygen, water to provide the most basic of chemical reactions which fire the entire process. We might wear shoes but we don't need them, and if we wear shoes we might wear socks to keep our feet from chafing. Some people might require canes or crutches to walk; most of us will at some point in our lives. But otherwise, what is needed to walk is quite minimal.

Compare this to what is needed for an automobile. A car requires roads, which require the felling of trees, the flattening of land, the diversion of streams, and the pouring of asphalt, which is petroleum tar mixed with bits of sand and rock. Cars also require gasoline or diesel, both of which are liquids created by electricity-intense refinement of raw petroleum pumped from the earth and then transported long distances before reaching the fuel tank of a car. And more: a car is constructed of plastics (again, petroleum), as well as steel and other composite metals gouged out of mountainsides or mining-pits and forged in energy-intense mills and refineries. All of that needs transporting yet again, by more petroleum products, to automobile factories where workers assemble them in electricity-intense environments. All of this happens before the car reaches an auto-lot, where it is then sold to people who save money earned from work to put down-payments on them and drive them home.

Walking causes remarkably little damage to the earth, while everything it takes to create and operate an automobile causes intense damage. Yet contained in one law, Pedestrian Interference With Traffic, is an entire upside-down political world-view which punishes the actions of a single human who might dare temporarily delay irrevocable destruction.

Everything that goes into creating an automobile makes profit for someone. The contractors who cut down the trees and who lay the asphalt, the oil companies who pump and refine the petroleum, the mining companies who rip metal from earth, the auto-makers who create the damn things and ask for government bail-outs when they don't make enough money, and all the other companies that exist as accessories to car-culture (gas stations, convenience stores, drive-through restaurants) have massive investments in the continuation of automobiles. Each also engages in destruction of the natural world in order to profit.

All of that destruction and all of that profit is maintained by a political order. So while there's nothing inherently political about walking, in this political order, jaywalking can be a revolutionary act. This is also why it's illegal.

## Politics and Anti-Politics

It's in this same way that witchcraft is political. It's political also because it is composed of human actions and embodied cultural memory from which the political system does not profit.

Because of this, it is also anti-political. To understand why, we must delve into a little word play. The words politics, policy, and police all derive from the same Greek word, *polis*. The *polis* was the city in its ideal, conceptual form. The Latin version of this word was *civitas*, from which we get the words civil, citizen, civics, city, and civilization. Both *polis* and *civitas* describe the same sort of formal existence, one where human laws, economic concerns, property, and punishment are all primary. So, the *polis* was not just the city, but the entire order it established, what we usually call "civilization."

Everything outside the polis was raw nature, wild, untamed, animal existence. Outside civilization are the barbarians, the heath-dwellers, wolves and other large predators, and the lawless women and men. Outside the polis were places the laws, the judges, the rulers and the concerns of the polis held no sway. Politicians could not make laws to govern the barbarians or the wolves because neither barbarians nor wolves recognize the authority of the *polis*.

Here there are two things we should remember. First, the word *paganus*, from which we derive the word Pagan, was an antonym of *civitas*, or as a friend likes to remind me, "Pagan meant red-neck in Latin."

Also, again, our word police comes from *polis*. Police is a noun and a verb. As a noun, it indicates those who "enforce the control of the community by the political order." Put another way, police are the agents of the *polis*. Police as a verb is similar and comes later. Police police; men and women perform the act of enforcing the political order. They ensure you act civil (according to the city), that you obey the laws of the *polis*, or are punished you when you act outside of the political order. This is what we call policing.

Let's return to that horrendous crime I mentioned earlier, that of Pedestrian Interference With Traffic. It is the will of the political order that a human not interfere with the movement of automobiles, and it is the police who would enforce that will. So, if I were to stand right now in an inter-section calling to an ancient goddess, the police might arrive to stop me. If they don't, and if I don't get hit by a car, then I have acted outside the political order with no repercussions. The moment the police do arrive, however, the *polis*, the political order, civilization, reassert themselves to say not only "thou shalt not" but "thou shall go to jail."

But jail for what, exactly? Interfering with cars? Or for interfering with the entire political order itself?

This is what I mean when I say that witchcraft is both political and anti-political. Witchcraft is a political act in a world where jaywalking is a re-volutionary act. Witchcraft is anti-political in that what we do often runs counter to the will of the political order.

Private property is a crucial location of this political/anti-political position of witchcraft. Private ownership of land means fences, walls, asphalt, con-crete. I cannot go talk to a particular tree if it is behind a fence; I cannot visit a particular grave if it is now below a parking lot. The tree behind that fence, the grave under the asphalt, and my own desire to visit either of them are therefore political, subject to politics. Likewise, jumping the fence or hammering through the pavement are both political acts.

The anti-political nature of witchcraft as it relates to private property is even more clear. Claiming that a tree must be open to all, that a grave should not be covered, and that I should be able to visit either without bar-riers is stating that the political order should have no power over those things. No one should get to own a tree, but the political order says other-wise. The dead shouldn't be covered by parking lots, but civilization says otherwise. And if I try to make either of those things true, the police will make sure the will of the *polis* is done. Thus, my witchcraft stands against the political order. It is anti-political specifically because the political order claims the right to control my actions.

So the politics of my witchcraft are the politics of revolution, the over-throw of the political order.

While witchcraft is both political and anti-political, it cannot be apolitical. It cannot simply ignore the political order, because that political order is destroying the earth. As Peter Grey wrote in *Apocalyptic Witchcraft*:

*"I have heard it said that a land wight does not care about the politics of who sum-mons it. This is a glib statement. It is politics which enables the destruction of the very land which the wight stands guard over. Man is a political animal, those who say that they stand outside of, or above politics are the esotericists whose clean hands are washed in the blood of those who have no choice but to put their hands in the ma-*

*chinery. Politics is not optional for First Nations, women, queers, blacks or any of the other slave classes. Abstention is a position of privilege which aids the pattern of destruction, arguing only for our impotence. There is no left-right dichotomy, there are those who are destroying the body, and those who stand against them. Economics is war by other means, and in this asymmetric war against life itself, you do not have the luxury of choice."*

The political order in which we live privileges the existence of cars over the survival of the land. It privileges all the profit derived from automobiles over the lives of forests, streams, animals, and even humans. Witchcraft is the jaywalker, the pedestrian interfering with traffic, the human who shrugs off the demands of the *polis* and the enforcement of the police in favor of the wild, unruled, uncivilized earth, even in the middle of a city.

The witch thus knows that the city is the core of the *polis*, the beating heart of civilization. And it's there the witch knows to strike deepest, where it is both strongest and most vulnerable. The busiest intersection is where the political order resides, and it's in those places we must start: from the crossroads.

## The Will of the *Polis*

Most witches are smart enough not to wander into intersections during the middle of rush-hour. And anyway, much of our activities are done at night, out of the prying eyes of mortals and away from the glare of traffic lights.

If some small part of you was thinking that interfering with traffic just sounds like a bad idea, we should explore that some more. Perhaps you were thinking, "but some people need to drive to work." It's true, of course. Many people do, and cars are the primary means for them to do so. But again, that work is defined by the political order. If you do not work, you cannot get money. Without money, you cannot pay rent or buy food. Without either a home or food, you cannot live.

All that, too, is defined by the political order under which we live, and the very fact that we understand that logic so well proves that we are thoroughly colonized by it. We are civilized, politicized subjects to the will of those for whom a jaywalker is a criminal but an automobile is a societal good. These are the same people for whom deforestation is an acceptable cost to build roads, and oil spills and climate change are mere unfortunate side-effects of that societal good.

We have internalized their thinking, which means we are their political subjects. I mean subjects here the same way we would speak about someone being subject to the king or that an area might be subject to frequent flooding. We are in a position of passivity and subservience, a place of being affected by forces over which we have little control.

The way that we have internalized the logic of civilisation, the logic of this political order, shows that we are political subjects. We measure our actions and temper our will according to this subjectivity. We don't usually cross the street illegally, we don't jump fences, we don't dig up the pavement.

But we are also more than just subjects of the *polis*. We are also the police of the *polis*. If you were to see a person standing in an intersection, blocking traffic, waving their arms wildly in the air, your first inclination is probably to call emergency services. If you happen to be driving and someone blocked traffic in this way, you're likely to curse at them for making you late for work. You'd call the police or maybe an ambulance, summoning the agents of the political order to handle the aberrancy, the outbreak of uncivilized, wild, unruly behavior.

You concern might even be completely honorable: perhaps the person is in a mental-health crisis, so by policing their actions you may think you are doing them a favor, maybe even saving their life. Regardless, you become the agent of the political order. You become the police who polices for the *polis*, the civil servant who performs their civic duty by making sure civilisation is protected.

At such a point, the *polis* is no longer just the political order, the *civitas* is no longer just civilisation. When they reproduce themselves within you, they have become something completely different, much stronger and harder to disentangle from the human in which they've merged.

They become Empire.

You become Empire.

When we talk of Empire, we usually think Rome, centurions, high civic pride, imperial conquest. Or perhaps we think Britain, God Saving the Queen, the international slave and tea trade, occupied India, colonial America. We could choose from many more: the French Empire under Napolean with its west-African and Caribbean subjugation. Or perhaps the U.S.S.R, all those client states under Soviet control.

Perhaps you even think of the United State of America, undoubtedly the most powerful empire the world has yet seen. A massive surveillance state, the oppression of Blacks and First Nations and immigrants, relentless foreign wars and occupations to secure an ever-dwindling oil supply, all that with a civic religion that would have been the envy of the architects of the Third Reich.

All those are Empires, each following similar trajectories from economic greatness to economic collapse. They've all crumbled except for the last on our list, and that one is undoubtedly collapsing as well. But the particular Empire in which find ourselves is not just one nation, but rather an entire Order of Meaning which privileges concerns of Capital, authority, and profit over the pedestrian concerns of the witch and the land which is the witch's lover.

We can feel the shape of Empire when we walk, when our feet are upon the earth. Empire prevents us with its borders and fences, it cuts through our heart with its highways and rails. Pavement shuts out our access to the soil in which our food and medicines might grow, while towers of steel and electric lighting (for "safety") blot out the stars from our view.

We can feel the shape of Empire, but we do not always name it. It names itself Liberal Democracy, Modernity, Civilization, Progress, all words we have been domesticated into believing mean "good." But it does not feel good when we walk through it, when we view through fences of chain-link or barbed wire a construction pit where once a forest stood, or regard shopping centers in seas of asphalt where once a meadow fruited flowers and herbs.

It likewise does not feel good to awake each day to drive over roads to meaningless work, nor to gather our food sealed in plastic packages from shelves in warehouses illuminated by the false light of florescence. It does not feel good to return to filing-cabinet apartments in cramped cities to an evening of catatonic half-slumber before glowing screens.

Modernity, Civilization, Capitalism, Liberal Democracy—these are all names for the un-speakable malaise our bodies feel, their grief at our divorce from the land, even more so when we are assured that all of this is "good." But let us call that malaise Empire, and remember that it is ending.

## "The End of History"

Empires have always tried to cheat death and this one is no different.

Empires always pompously declare themselves eternal. The British swore the sun would never set on them, the Third Reich was supposed to last 1000 years. It is mere propaganda; the crone who stands at the gates of death can never be denied.

Western Democratic Capitalist Empire has likewise declared itself eternal. Citing the fall of Fascist governments in Spain, Italy, and Germany, as well as the failure of Soviet-style State Communism, Liberal ideologues and technocrats asserted that Capitalism and Democratic forms of government were the destiny of humanity, the final stage of human development.

Though originating from the priests and politicians of the archonic order of Empire, this story has filtered down to the rest of us. The Order of Meaning into which our lives are set as stars lacking constellations appears to us thus as immutable, always-already existing, eternal.

Empire seems not only to have won, but to have never needed to wage war against the earth in the first place. Like the Calvinist cosmology from which Empire's narrative sprung, all the earth and the peoples in it seem naturally-fit for consumption and submission, our classes and roles pre-ordained, our lives pre-destined.

But the persistance of this narrative shows Empire's weakness. Staggering amounts of money are spent to remind us that Capital is unassailable, that resistance is futile, rebellion foolish, opposition fatal. Children must be told that magic and gods are only stories and witches only fictions. But children can be forgiven their naive faith in bitter, discenchanted elders; we, infantilized, passive subjects of Empire have no excuse.

Empire's propaganda is counter-revolution: attempts to close breached walls, repair the invisible net which screens out from us our power. Empire must conceal from us our history, speak to us of itself as history's end. Empire does not wish us to know it was born, for all that was born must die. To be bornless is to be deathless, and Empire is neither.

This Empire under which we all suffer, under whom we are all ruled, was born upon the factory floor and upon the witch's stake. And in the char of those burnings and the soot from the smokestacks we can see its end.

Industrialised capitalism started in England around 1760. Before then, there were no factories, no coal powered mills, no rail, no highways. Before then, everything humans used was made by humans or raw from the earth, none of it with the input of fossil fuels.

The first coal-fired factories were built in cities swollen with refugees from the surrounding areas, refugees recently severed from the land through the fences of Enclosure. No longer could they raise animals and plants from the earth with their own two feet firmly planted on the ground; now, their only option was to stand on wood and stone factory floors for 14 hours a day in William Blake's "Satanic Mills."

# Witches In A Crumbling Empire

Humans are hard to control. Humans don't like working all day for someone else. They have to eat, and piss, and shit, and rest. Many women bleed every moon, sometimes they get pregnant and have to care for their children. But coal doesn't tire. Coal doesn't show up to work late after a night of drinking or fucking. Coal doesn't need a rest, doesn't get menstrual cramps, doesn't daydream about how life can be better. Coal also doesn't demand wages.

So the great "revolution" of industrialisation began with the turning of human into machine and the slow replacement of human labor with black carbon labor from the earth. In the Americas, the people called Black were also used to replace waged labor. In both cases, the rich tried to find a low-cost, easily-managed, fully-predictable means to gain wealth.

Yet coal and oil blacken the cities and skies with soot. The Capitalists darkened the skies with their greed, then found such staining uncomely and sough ways to hide that blackness. Where filters upon smokestacks could not suffice, they moved factories where their putrid defecation might no longer be hidden to all except the poor too desperate or defeated to complain.

Like covering a necrotic wound, masking the uglyness of industry only postponed the disease. Now oceans rise and forests burn, water tables deplete and species die.

Though Empire could ignore for a few centuries its destruction of the realms it rules, it could never so easily ignore the tendency of humans to revolt against their masters, be they slaves or peasants, workers or servants. Humans don't make very good machines: we are unpredictable, tire easily, and anyway would rather be creating art or eating or fucking than doing monotonous work for little pay.

So it was that the same era which saw the birth of industrialised Capitalism also saw the birth of all modern forms of government and control: the modern city, the nation-state, Democracy, representative government, prisons resembling factories (resembling schools, resembling prisons). It also saw the birth of the modern police and the political order under which we now live, which we call Empire.

## By Empire

By Empire I mean America, but I also do not.

By Empire I mean Capitalism, but I also do not.

By Empire I mean colonization. I mean industrialisation. I mean the slaughter of indigenous peoples and the enslavement of Africans. I mean the carbon in the air and the worker in the factory. I mean all the newly extinct species and all the dying forests. I mean the corporations which own the internet and the corporations who profit from the computers and smartphones to which we are all enchained.

By Empire, I mean the foreign wars. I mean an Arab woman cradling the corpse of her decapitated daughter and shaking her fist at the gay Black dude from Los Angeles who only joined the Army to get money to support his mother.

By Empire, I mean the Mexican child screaming as her father is taken away by an ICE agent whose grandparents fled the Nazi advance in Europe.

By Empire, I mean the Black father mourning his son killed by a cop whose ancestors sold themselves into indentured servitude rather than starve to death during the famine in Ireland.

By Empire, I mean the intersectional feminist writing essays about the exploitation of women and children on a computer made through the exploitation of Asian women and African children.

By Empire I mean the Arab man who massacres gays in a nightclub to retaliate for atrocities none of those people committed.

By Empire, I mean the single white mother driving her disabled kid to a doctor's appointment over roads lain by migrant workers who are about to get deported.

By Empire I mean the *civitas* and the *polis*. I mean civilization and the police, the laws and logic, the political order, the thou shalt nots and the prisons where you go when you refuse to listen.

But more than anything, I mean the Empire in each of you and the Empire in me. I mean all that was once wild and raw and sacred in us that is now ground into machine-parts and mechanical obedience. By Empire I mean you, and by Empire I mean me.

And finally, by Empire I mean this thing that is crumbling around us, gasping for air, begging us to keep it alive.

## The Factory Floor & The Witch's Stake

The Empire that is crumbling around us was born on the factory floors and the witch's stake, and both were assaults on the human body. Silvia Federici said it, in her essay *"In Praise of the Dancing Body:"*

*Capitalism was born from the separation of people from the land and its first task was to make work independent of the seasons and to lengthen the workday beyond the*

# Witches In A Crumbling Empire

*limits of our endurance.... What we have not always seen is what the separation from the land and nature has meant for our body, which has been pauperized and stripped of the powers that pre-capitalist populations attributed to it.*

If the first task of Capitalism was to separate us from land and nature, they have more than succeeded. One need only look at the vastly artificial surroundings we all live in, the devices we use to speak with each other, the manufactured foods and synthetic medicines. Can you walk outside your home and find something edible growing by the pavement? Do you know which birds share your neighborhood with you? Can you point to where precisely the sun will rise tomorrow morning without a compass? Without looking outside tonight or at the internet, which phase is the moon in?

But it's useless to rail against this disconnection. What separates us from the land and nature is not a current assault in an ongoing struggle: the war was won by them long ago. We are an occupied people, often occupying occupied land cleared long before any of us were born. If that war was lost, though, the other war is still on going. Says Federici again:

*Mechanization—the turning of the body, male and female, into a machine—has been one of capitalism's most relentless pursuits.*

Capitalism has needed us to act like machines so we can fit into the system as mere, fully-interchangeable cogs. Many of use don't fit, though: be it our bodies themselves or our failure to conform, the process of turning us into machines is never fully complete.

Consider the countless technological distractions and institutions which have helped us forget our bodies and trained us to act like machines: the masturbatory fantasies of video games and pornography, the medicalisation of any bodily refusal to be a good worker. Gyms look like factories for a reason, for it's in the mills and on the mechanical looms where we first lost the meaning of muscle and blood. And then there is clock time, our smartphones and alarm clocks, schools which teach kids to move from class to class to prepare them to move from task to task.

Capitalism needed to separate us from the land and our body because it is the land and the body which tells you this is all wrong. The land screams as species go extinct, forests die, icecaps melt. Your body screams when you treat it as a machine.

Your body tells you this is all wrong. Starting from the body, you know you tire faster when you are doing meaningless work. You know the food on offer to you at the supermarkets is empty, you know that the air you breathe is often toxic. You know sitting for eight hours staring at a screen hurts more than just your eyes, that standing behind a counter slinging coffee to exhausted people makes you a poorly-paid drug dealer. All that knowledge is what Capitalism needs you not to know. All those feelings are what Empire fears you'll feel.

Capitalism needed to separate us from the land and our bodies for another reason. Your body is always in contact with something else, something outside yourself. Your feet, the lowest part of you, the easiest part to ignore until they hurt, they connect to the entire world-soul. Taking your shoes off, standing on the grass or the sand or stone, you become no longer a machine but a body again, part of something always bigger than yourself, with a different logic, a more intuitive time, a deeper truth.

Your feet on the earth, you cannot be disconnected from the earth and the seasons, because you are also the earth and its seasons. Work in summer is not work in winter, the time of your waking and the cycles of your sleeping follow a different rhythm fully separate from the time of money-making, the time of machines. Capitalism needs you to forget this.

Witchcraft tells you to remember. Empire was born on the factory floor, and it was also born on the witch's stake. Failure to file down our rough bits, refusal to conform to the will of the political order, speaking into the darkness and hearing it answer back, and worst of all encouraging others to do the same lands us at best in jail, or riddled with mental-illnesses that were non-existent in pre-capitalist lands.

Capitalism needed to separate us from the land and our bodies, Empire needed us to become passive subjects of the political order.

Passivity is not receptivity. As a gay man I can assure you more action goes into receptive sex than merely closing your eyes and thinking about the Empire. I suspect most women would concur. Receptivity opens us to the world of senses, of feelings, of meaning. You are being receptive now, taking my words into you, playing with them, weaving their meaning into the tapestry of you. But passivity makes you a victim, a mere tool in the hands of the powerful. Passivity is consumption, selection between lifestyle options, an identity defined not by what you do but by what you choose. Did you vote Democrat or Republican? Drink Coke or Pepsi? Use an iPhone or Android?

Passivity reduces will to mere consumer preference. No longer will to power but a mere checkbox on a ballot or a selection on a screen. No longer desire and suffering but mere distractions to dull the fatigue of work and the anxiety of alienation.

# Witches In A Crumbling Empire

You cannot force someone to become passive except by long applications of torture. But there is another route, a slower one, by which you can conquer the will of others by telling them not "thou shalt not" but "thou cannot." Like the God of Eden's lies to the woman in the garden, we are told we cannot survive without Capitalism, cannot be safe without police, cannot find meaning outside of waged work, cannot find love without cosmetics.

And so what we did not lose on the factory floor we lost with the death of witches. Not only the women with herbs and poison roots, not only the crones bearing stories from times before private property, not only the maidens urging worship in temples of wild lust, not only the mothers feeding us from their bodies. Not only them, but also them: the women who reminded us an entire world can be made not from city and machine but forest and dirt.

Not only them, but also the heretics, the mad, the dreamers, the rebels. The men dressed like women tearing down fences along with women drest like men, refusing the enclosure of the sacred commons and the seizure of land for the profit of the few. The indigenous elders gunned down by settlers, the traditional healers dead in the hulls of slave ships. All of them taught what Empire needed us to forget: the earth knows what the computer never will, and the body bleeds a liquid more powerful than petroleum.

With them gone, we started to believe we can-not. We cannot heal ourselves without pharmaceuticals, we cannot feed ourselves without factory farms. We cannot make our own clothes, cannot craft our own homes. We must now suckle at the toxic teat of the Market while it slaps us with an invisible hand. We started to believe we cannot resist.

In the screaming defiance of the immolated witches was a reminder: we can refuse to submit, even in death. It took centuries to shape us into what we are now, passive sniveling subjects of Empire and Capital. Though this may seem long, we lived outside Empire much longer. Capitalism is new and short-lived, compared even to Feudalism. It differs only in its full permeation of all our existence, and it is for this reason we call it Empire.

## Empire is Collapsing

Though Empire tried to hide the stain of its use of fossil fuels, the climate change caused by Capitalism cannot be stopped any longer. Its effects already cause famines and resource wars throughout the world.

Between 30,000 and 140,000 species go extinct every year now; at the beginning of the 1800's, this number was no more than 1000 yearly. Cities are beginning to flood, water tables depleting, while the oil-wells which make the entire Empire run are going dry. Climate change will increase the refugee crises currently fueling the nationalist parties in Europe and the US, and whether they are fleeing from resource wars or unmanned drone bombers, they are undoubtedly the first quakes of Empire's impending collapse.

Empire has tried to deny death, but the crone that stands on the other side of death's door revealed her trump card. Some in the heart of Empire still cling to the vain hope that Donald Trump or the rise of other nationalist figures are merely unfortunate set-backs to the progress of civilization. But these are not mere reversals of Empire's progress, they are Empire trying to save itself.

With the eyes of a witch we can see past the obvious racism and nationalist rhetoric of new border policies to see the architects of Empire's terrified glance at what is coming. The droughts of climate change bring floods of climate refugees; xenophobic hysteria, increased border security—the engineers are attempting to shore up the ruins of Empire.

Likewise, the rise of new surveillance apparatuses, the permeation of Capitalist social media into our every interaction, the militarization of police forces. The Capitalists know better than we do the power we hold in our hands and prepare, raising again stakes, piling faggots beneath them, terrified of the moment witches rise up to lead the people in revolt.

That time is not yet, and will not come until the charlatans who claim to lead us are silenced. They who speak to us of acceptance spit upon the torment of our ancestors. To accept what is around us now, to call such things "good" and "necessary," is to laugh in the faces of the screaming witches who died so this Empire could arise. To chase after like mongrel dogs the trinkets and crumbs the Capitalists throw down to us on the floor, the "rights" and "freedoms" and all the glossy junk cluttering store shelves, is to jeer at the sorrow and sufferings of our ancestors hauled to work in chains or prodded into mills by the terror of starvation.

To accept Empire is to deny the dead, the tortured witches of our past and the tortured rebels dying in Empire's prisons. To not fight Empire is to defy our own bodies, defile the land and destroy the bodies of others. To accept Empire is to become Empire.

To fight Empire is to stare in the face of our own deaths and laugh, knowing the worst that might happen is Empire might burn us, too. But to the witches who risked the stake to avoid forever the factory floor, the in-surrectionists who risked bullets to forever avoid submission, and any who risked the rage of Empire for the possibility that Empire might fall, the choice was an easy one. So is ours.

We cannot undo what has already been done. We cannot resurrect the dead witches, tear their charred corpses off the burnt stakes, nor can we re-trieve the mangled bodies of children from the steam-powered looms in England. We cannot bring the species we've lost back, nor can we pull all that carbon out of the air. We cannot undo the slaughter of indigenous peoples, we cannot bring the ice caps back.

To keep itself alive, Empire has brought death to others. As Empire stands at the gates of its own death, we stand it with, peering through to the other side, greeting those who come to meet us.

Witches know death well. The writer Peter Grey, in his essay *"Rewilding Witchcraft,"* put it this way:

*Some will be afraid of this knowledge; witchcraft should be liberated by it, liberated from petty concerns to pursue lives of beauty, liberated from the sleepwalking into death that our culture has made for us and our children. So I counsel, confront death. For witchcraft to be anything other than the empty escapism of the socially dysfunctional or nostalgia for bygone ages, it needs to feel the shape of its skull, venerate the dead and the sacred art of living and dying with meaning. We are all on the fierce path now.*

And later in that same essay:

*We need to offer the death rites in a culture that pretends that death can be cheated by buying the latest i-gadget or hooking ourselves up to plasma bags of young blood. These technological and scientific responses do not account for the wider environment which we do not control, but which now seeks to redress the killing balance and is do-ing so with storm surge and wildfire and tornado and flood and drought regardless of what is playing on your headphones or how high the gates are to your compound. I welcome this storm.*

As death comes for Empire, it is for us witches to sharpen our blades. No longer can we pretend to enjoy the fruits of capitalist exploitation of the earth, no longer can we beg on our knees for recognition and protection from false-faced politicians and the machine-will of the *polis.*

We are hardly the only ones to notice that Empire is faltering. The na-tionalists with their false histories and the progressive fantasists with their false messianic futures scream about an "endangered way of life." They are correct, and it is time it is endangered. The way of life they wish to preserve slaughters species, poisons the air, and grinds human life into dust. It is time that it be not only endangered, but that it go extinct.

We can find no allies amongst them. We desire nothing less than the death of Empire and all its forms. We will not sup at their tables nor march along with their attempt to rally Empire against its inevitable end. The signs we wave into the air are not slogans to make this world better but invocations to summon another world.

## Against The Machines

Empire made us into subjects, Capitalism made us machines. But regardless of how much power either has over us, the simplest truth is that we are neither.

We must remove all machine language from the way we describe ourselves, and extend that favor to others. Our bodies are not machines. We do not process information, we do not store memories, we do not burn fuel. The tepid might object: these are mere metaphors, useful for describing things. But poets, bards, priests, therapists, and advertisers all know something the rest of us are prone to forget: metaphor is magic, and not all magic is good.

To that point, we must examine the magic which founded this dying Empire. Consider the words used by Francis Bacon, John Dee's student and an architect of the mechanistic worldview under which Capitalism thrives, to describe the place of nature and the role of the man of science:

> *…hound nature in her wanderings, and you will be able when you like to lead and drive her afterwards to the same place again. Neither ought a man to make scruple of entering and penetrating into those holes and corners when the inquisition of truth is his whole object.*

Painting nature as a women to be raped, "entering and penetrating" her holes, was more than a mere description of the industrialist's task. It was, if anything, the magical theory under which they operate. The inventor of the steam engine described his task the same way, defining nature as an intractable woman who must be forced into doing what her master commands.

Describing your body as a machine reproduces Capitalism's desire for you to be a machine. It affects not only how you see your body, but also how you treat it. Another quote from Silvia Federici's essay *"In Praise of the Dancing Body"*:

> *In our time, models for the body are the computer and the genetic code, crafting a dematerialized, dis-aggregated body, imagined as a conglomerate of cells and genes*

*each with her own program, indifferent to the rest and to the good of the body as a whole. Such is the theory of the 'selfish gene,' the idea, that is, that the body is made of individualistic cells and genes all pursuing their program a perfect metaphor of the neo-liberal conception of life, where market dominance turns against not only group solidarity but solidarity with own ourselves. Consistently, the body disintegrates into an assemblage of selfish genes, each striving to achieve its selfish goals, indifferent to the interest of the rest.*

*To the extent that we internalize this view, we internalize the most profound experience of self-alienation, as we confront not only a great beast that does not obey our orders, but a host of micro-enemies that are planted right into our own body, ready to attack us at any moment. Industries have been built on the fears that this conception of the body generates, putting us at the mercy of forces that we do not control. Inevitably, if we internalize this view, we do not taste good to ourselves. In fact, our body scares us, and we do not listen to it.*

The body is not our enemy, an intractable machine always prone to breaking down. Your body is you, you are your body. Your body is the only way you experience the world. It is how you know love and pain, hunger and safety.

As we stop describing ourselves as machines, we then begin to see the machines which regulate our existence. No greater machine enemy of the body is there than machine-time, the clock. Under the regime of machine-time, we wake not when we are rested but when we must go to work. We sleep not when we are tired but when the clocks says we must. We judge experiences by the clock: that was a good hour spent, those were two hours wasted.

The time of Empire is the time of machines. The time of witchcraft is the time of the body which is the time of the earth and the moon. Women who menstruate know this truth particularly well. From Niki Whiting's essay, *"My Resistance Will Be Bloody."*

*I resist Capitalism by not being "productive." I resist by refusing to accept that my body or your body is a machine. Our bodies need to rest. Our bodies need time and space to heal, to purge, to grow, to be. Honoring my body shows my kids that the female body is not disgusting, but a cause for celebration.*

*Blood is life. The blood that pumps in my body and your body every moment of every day is life. Your heart's blood and my cunt's blood. A bleeding woman is a powerful woman. A bleeding woman can grow a life in the hidden spaces of her body. A woman who resists hiding her power, in her sex, in her blood, lays bare her connection to the sacrality of life, of our flesh.*

## What Thou Wilt...

While the capitalists convinced us we are machines rather than bodies, Empire convinced us we were passive, will-less subjects. The next magic after reclaiming our body is to reclaim our will. This is easier than becoming a body again, but you cannot attain it until you are a body.

Empire tells us not only "thou shalt not" but also "thou cannot." This latter lie we must fight at ever turn.

When we are told we cannot grow our own food, we must grow our food. When we are told we cannot survive without money, we must survive without money. When we are told we cannot be safe without the police, we must become safe without the police.

There is great risk here. The body reclaimed in a powerful thing, but the will reclaimed is a dangerous thing. The opposite of passive subjectivity is engaged activity; we begin doing rather than always being done to, and this must mean fighting back when we are harmed. We are not supposed to fight back. We are told we must rely on political systems of justice, or on karma. Or when we are harmed, we are supposed to bear the pain inside us, go to therapy to resolve the misery of capitalist existence.

Can't wake up on time for work? Experience anxiety when you think about your bills or your taxes? Get depressed and can't seem to enjoy all the things your job lets you buy? You can ease the pain of living with what Capitalism has to sell, but you can never stop its source that way. You can fight for bits of freedom, but you can never liberate much more than a little more space for yourself.

When you become a body again, you can trace that pain back, sometimes to individuals, and then to systems of control. Keep tracing, keep following the tendrils past those systems, the patriarchy or racism, colonization or ablism, and you come to the true source, the center holding it all together.

No education will heal racism until the Empire which reproduces it is destroyed. No legislation will overthrow the Patriarchy until the Empire which establishes it falls away. And Empire can never die until we refuse to be its subject.

Once you embrace your will and refuse to obey, others will join you. Be warned: when a community rises to defend itself, they become a threat to the political order. Consider Standing Rock. Tribes who have fought for decades and even centuries uniting on a desolate plain to stop a small section of pipeline being laid: such solidarity is the very opposite of passive subjectivity and a direct confrontation of Empire's power, and it for this reason it was crushed.

Empire needs us to write letters to the editor and call your senator. Empire needs you to tick someone's box in a voting booth, to wave powerless slogans in the air, to donate to a charity, and to press "like" on a social media post. It needs you to consume democracy, not enact it.

The path from here to there is difficult, but it does not start with massive protests and camps of defiance. Instead, it starts in the body and an open declaration of war against "thou cannot." What have you been taught you cannot do with your body that you never questioned? What lies did you accept about your power that you passively accepted?

This is not an easy path. In fact, it can be one of extreme pain. Are you an introvert, or have you told yourself you are not good around people? Is the mental trauma of capitalist alienation causing you sorrow, or have you been told you are clinically depressed?

Our language around our bodies has been colonized by machine-will, our certainties of our limits shaped by Empire's fear of our power. To fit into the regime of Liberal Democratic "rights," we have abdicated our will. To deserve not to die because we desire certain bodies over others we have needed to hide behind determinism, claiming that secular god Biology caused us to be gay or reject assigned genders. To deserve not to starve and have our bodies mangled in relentless work, we have needed to claim mental and physical disabilities as our defense.

The greater and more terrifying magic is to re-assert our wills. It is not that we *cannot* work for the Capitalists, but that *we refuse to*. It is not that we have no choice in whom we desire or the expressions of our bodies, but that we choose to manifest our will against Empire's "thou shalt nots."

## The Land's Embrace

To reclaim our wills and to deny that our bodies are machines but rather things of flesh, bone, shit, skin, semen and piss, an inescapable truth arises: the body will die. We are our bodies, so we will die.

By abandoning machine-thinking, we are forced to confront our death and decay. Machines don't die, they just break down. Your body will die, as will mine. And just as you and I shall die, so too will Empire.

We reclaim our bodies. We reclaim our will. Only from here can we then reclaim our place in the land, and power it grants us.

Ask: why did Capitalism need to separate us from the land? Why does Empire slay forests and lay down asphalt? Why are we shunted into tiny dwellings from trees, why are rivers and streams buried under pavement?

We were told we were machines so we could work in factories. We were told we cannot do for ourselves so that we would rely on Empire.

We were separated from the land so we would have no place to escape.

When we stand with our feet on the earth, we remember we are part of it. We are an animal, we are beings of will, and we are wild, unruly, uncivilized things which belong everywhere.

We transgress. We trespass. We put our bodies where we are told they are not supposed to be, because we know we belong everywhere the world is. Borders cannot stop us, fences only slow us down. Prisons and schools and offices are there to restrain us: we will not be restrained.

There is no greater teacher, no more powerful ally, no more loving guide than the land. Through our feet we connect to the soul of the world and all who live in it. We are always already connected to the land, but Empire needs us to forget.

Our food comes from there. Our air is breathed out by forests and plankton, our water comes from the sky and from below the ground. All we need is the land, and all we are is the land. Remember this, and you cannot abide its destruction. Remember this, and you become, as in the words of Peter Grey, the witch "created by the land to speak and act for it."

That is the simple mystery. There are others. There is the magic of shapeshifting, not just taking on the form of animals, but that of the land itself. In a vale between two mountains in Snowdon, on the shores of the lake where Ceridwen sought the recipe for Awen, on a cliff where the Red and White Dragons were uncovered by Merlin, I learned this mystery. I became at once the rain falling upon me, the rain passing through me, the stones soaked under my feet, the water in my boots, the lake before me, the rivers below the ground, and the sky crying the rain into the land.

I have been this elsewhere. It is easiest when there is the least amount of concrete, where nature still can be a bit raw, a bit naked. In places like this, you must also be a bit raw and a bit naked. You are having sex with the land, the land is having sex with you. When you are done, when the spirits of the land have thrust their orgasm into your soul, you know what the land needs. It also knows you, takes a part of you with it as it recedes behind you when you leave. It is like any lover: you are both changed.

# Witches In A Crumbling Empire

If Capitalism needed to divorce us from the land, then we were once married to it. We must become married to it again, seeking out its desires, following its lead. Against Francis Bacon's fantasy of raping nature, we must seek to be its lover. Here, more than anything, the receptivity of which we earlier spoke is key. We must be nature's whore.

## Seeing Through The Veil

I have told you what Empire is, and what it made of us. How we forgot we are bodies and not machines, forgot we have will and are not mere subjects. How we were separated from the land, fenced off, forbidden, excluded.

I have told you how to remember, how to fight the machine by becoming bodies again, how to fight "thou cannot" by trying to anyways. And I have told you how to shrug off the prisons of Empire by escaping into the land of which you are composed.

This is all witchcraft, perhaps the only witchcraft that matters.

There is one more magic I will impart, the last weapon I know how to wield against Empire.

Empire exists with our help. It hides and reproduces itself in our actions. Each time we call the police, Empire lives again. Each moment we obey a law, Empire breathes more power.

An Empire dies when it can no longer exert power over others. When its subjects are no longer subjects, it cannot enforce its will. That is, an Empire will die when there is no one to do its will, to police the political order for it.

The slogan of Donald Trump's election campaign reveals the magic command of a dying Empire: "Make America Great Again." It is the voice of a dying nation, screaming from its deathbed, marshalling its last forces to its side. It shouts at us, "Make Me Again."

It is we who reproduce Empire. It is we are propping it up as it falls. It is we who shore up its ruins, patch up its leaks, hold up its falling pillars.

We can also do nothing at all, taking as many of those we love away from the toppling stones and plummeting beaes.

But we're witches. We know death, because we walk along its threshold, we stroll its borders, we commune with its denizens.

For some of us, it will be enough to know Empire is crumbling. They who have been gathering seeds to plant in the empty lots, kindling to light fires in the crossroads. To them we must say thank you. We will need gardens and celebrations in the ruins.

Some of us have also been gathering roots and herbs, learning poisons and curses. They are sharpening their knives under the moon's white glow, mixing ashes with blood and semen, throwing bones over graves and calling to spirits who are eager to help Empire fall. To them must also say thank you, and offer our aid.

The rest of us must choose to act, and quickly, for Empire has summoned its shadow, its final defenders. They who begin to march, proclaiming the birth of a new greatness. It is the same tired greatness that died in a bunker below Berlin, that slaughtered 10 million people with machine-like precision in prison factory camps. It is the same tired greatness that torched witches and tortured heretics in centuries past. They, whose propaganda has never relied upon the uncomfortable obstacle of truth, now arise everywhere to fight us, to blind those whose eyes are only now opening, to begin the sacrifices anew.

Our last weapon, our best weapon, is the magic of unveiling. We must see past what things appear to be to what they are. Chicanery, sleight-of-hand, illusion: these are not just the magic of the fraudster, but of the political order itself. Each convince the victim to assume only appearances, to look away from the switch through distraction. The bigger the spectacle, the easier it is to fool the observer. The flashier the performance, the harder it is to see what really happened.

We must look with our bodies, not just our eyes. We must see with the land, not what is shown to us by the backlit screens. We are animals, and animals can sense intent. When we return to the lowest part of our senses we can see through disguises. Feel with your back, with all that is behind you, not just what it is before.

The masses of refugees know what Empire tries to hide from view. Parts of the earth are dying, seas rising, droughts making land infertile. Animals know to move to better places when the resources run out. We are animals. We migrate, we follow the seasons and the food. Animals know when great danger has awakened in an area; we are no different, except that we have been taught not to listen to our animal nature.

Feel with your body where the danger is, and do not deny its warnings. Seek those who teach the knowledge of the body, how to read again its language. Many but not all those teachers are human. Many are plants, especially the forbidden ones. Many are ancestors, many are spirits, some are gods.

# Witches In A Crumbling Empire

Most of all, seek those who can teach you most about your body and theirs. The magic of love is foremost a magic of the body, manifested best through sex. In sex we remember desire arising from within us, rather than inscribed upon us by Empire's priests of publicity.

In sex we remember we are bleeding, shitting, sweating, dying and yet ever-living beasts, rutting in passions that cannot be sold to us and never be fully taken away. Amongst the crimes of the heretic and the witch, our un-couth, unclean, and unruly lusts have always been the most hideous to our judges and executioners. The sodomite, the whore: Empire correctly fears them.

In love, in sex, we learn not only the unboundaried nature of our own desires but the limitlessness of our lovers'. We learn to desire new things, whet and reforge our own in the fires of others, and most of all learn how desire can expand to encompass entire worlds and birth new ones. We learn the power of our bodies, our capacity for joy outside the markets and artificial spaces created to contain us.

And in love and in sex we learn no longer to fear death. The orgasm is *le petit mort* for a reason, and sex is death we never enter alone. In sex we learn that all which can ever be taken from us by Empire is our life, and the glimpses through the gates of death in sex grant visions to sustain us when Empire threatens to speed our course.

Empire's fear of its own death has made us fear our own. Its promises to extend our lives, keep us safe from suffering, and one day even conquer death itself are the lies it tells to itself, lies it needs us to believe. It is the terror of the body that has never surrendered to the love of another, the panicked fear of the impotent king.

We have no need of such fear. We surrender to the body, to the land, to the lover; we one day surrender also to death. Uncivilized, feral, embracing the will, marrying the land, fully again a body, we become witches as this Empire falters, gasping for air, crumbling, dying.

We become witches that help it die.

# I Told You I Have Always Known You

The sun had begun to slant early autumn light on your face, and in that illumination, gold and rose, I saw you for the first time.

I mean really saw you, unlike every other glance before when you spoke and I thought I heard but hadn't, that late afternoon before you had to leave and I wasn't sure I'd ever see you again.

The sun had begun to slant, showing me things I had never seen about you, things I never knew lay behind your eyes, behind your awkward laugh when I told you I thought you were beautiful all those other times before.

That's why you were laughing all those times before, because you knew I had not really yet seen you, was only uttering words I knew I was supposed to say, the sounds a man makes when he knows he's supposed to see something but isn't sure he did.

You were laughing because you knew I hadn't seen you yet.

And now I understand why, when you left just after the trees swallowed that last bit of light (just before everything went so very crimson and so very rose) your laughter changed.

I felt it, not so awkward, like you'd caught something in the light too when I said you were beautiful.

# Witches In A Crumbling Empire

You laughed and looked at me, turning your face so I could see. That's when I saw it, what I had never seen before behind your eyes, something for which the word beautiful was just man-noise.

Which is why you were always laughing before. And I said it anyway, and you laughed but it changed, and you stared at me like you saw something there too.

And then I said I love you, and then you did too.

And then I understood why you were always laughing.

And I think you understood why I always said you were beautiful.

And then you left, stood up as the trees swallowed the sun.

And then you left, and I did not know if I would ever see you again.

And then you left, and I held on to this love letter, written before we ever met, written now, remembering a future which will one day be a past in which I have always known you.

I still do not know if I will ever see you again, because I have not yet even seen you yet.

But I think I will, because I have this letter written before we ever met.

And if I do, I will show it to you.

"See?" I'll say.

"I told you I have always known you."

# *Like Water*

Tonight I sat drunk on the ledge of a bridge over a canal to listen to the water, to see if it had words or wisdom for me. But that is not fully true. I am writing this from that ledge over the canal listening to the water as I write, thinking about you.

What the water is telling me I cannot really hear. I think it is telling me to write you, or maybe just reminding me that life flows, cascades from the sky into the ground and our souls like love. That it's all much easier than we men make it: you just be, you fall, flow, soak into the earth and then rise again as clouds to fall again.

Water is the wisdom of women or the very rare very strong men, maybe. I wish I were that wise.

I wonder if a woman, or the water, or very strong men would know how to hold the feelings I have? Or maybe they would not hold them at all, but let them be, let them go where they want and need to go?

I wish I were more like them, like women or very strong men or like water. Maybe if I were I could tell you that I am falling into you like water falls over rocks, cascades from the sky, drips like rain from branches.

Instead I just sit on this bridge thinking of you, listening to the water, writing about what I would say if I could understand what it was telling me.

# *The Flood*

*For Seb Barnett*

It was a long day at work, a long week. You were so tired this morning you left your phone at home, too, so there was nothing to help distract you from how much you hate your job.

But it's Friday, and you're done for the week. You can breathe a little, maybe even go have a drink with friends.

You arrive home. You climb the steps to your apartment building. Some days, those two flights to your apartment seem daunting. Today's one of those days.

You hear the old couple on the first floor fighting about something through their door. They're always fighting, sometimes so much you have to crank your music up really loud to drown them out. It's gonna be one of those days, too.

When you get to your apartment though, you see the door's been left partially open. "Dammit," you mutter. You've asked your roommates repeatedly to not do that—it makes you feel unsafe. They should respect that. You don't want to yell at them, but...fuck.

When you push the door open you see the flood. Water's everywhere, literally pouring in streams from the ceiling over everything.

# The Flood

You moan as you look at your bedroom: Your mattress is soaked, your computer is sitting in a lake on your desk, all your favorite books on their shelves are bloated with wet pages. And then you remember—you left your phone plugged in by your bed, and there it is, sitting in a puddle of water.

You grab it, pick it up, and water spills out from its case.

Now you're shouting profanities. You survey the rest of the damage and start crying. You can't help yourself—it's all so much. You run to the living room to look at the painting your friend did for you last year. It's warped, destroyed. You cry again… they committed suicide a few months ago, that was the last thing you had from them.

You search the rest of the apartment quickly—the same damage in the other rooms, your roommates' bedrooms just as flooded.

It's all so much, too much.

You want to sit down, hold your head in your hands and weep. But there's nowhere dry to sit—your couch is sopping wet and water is still pouring from the ceiling above it.

Coming to your senses, staring at the ceiling, you realise the water's probably still running upstairs. You bolt out your door, tear up the stairwell with rage and pound on your upstairs' neighbour's door.

He opens it as you stand there, water flowing over your feet.

"Your apartment's flooding" you shout at him.

He nods, then hands you a wet dishtowel. "Yeah. Want to help us mop it up?"

One of your roommates is already inside with him. She looks at you, exasperated, holding a sponge and a bucket. "It's so awful!" she says, her voice shaking, tears streaming from her eyes. "Everything's ruined."

You look at the sponge in her hand, and the thin dishtowel in his hand and shake your head. "Don't you have a mop?" you ask, exasperated.

He shakes his head. "Couldn't be bothered. Those are expensive."

You resist the urge to punch him for being so dense, and then run back downstairs to your own apartment. You try not to look at all the damage, try to resist the urge to scream again. You grab your mop, a bucket, and a few already-soaked towels from the bathroom, and just as you are about to go back upstairs, your other roommate arrives home.

"It's coming from upstairs," you tell her. You hand her a towel, and start to walk past her before she stops you.

"We need to clean this first," she says.

"What? No—we have to stop the water from coming in."

"This is more urgent," she says. "My girlfriend's coming over tonight. We can clean this first and then stop the water coming in later."

"Are you serious?" you say, and then see her face. She's in shock, just as you were. She's not thinking clearly. And she's already gone into her bedroom and is trying to sop up water with the wet towels.

You try again. "We need to stop the water coming in first."

She acts like she didn't hear you. You say it one more time.

"We can't just ignore all this water," she finally says. "And I'm not helping that guy upstairs—he's an asshole" and then shuts her door, leaving you in the hallway with the mop bucket.

She's right. The guy's awful. But you shake your head and run back upstairs anyway. The door's open, and you enter to find both your roommate and your neighbor arguing and not cleaning up the water. She's decided now is the time to talk about how loud he is when he has sex; he counters that she's too sensitive and then starts complaining about the noise from her birthday party last month.

For a moment, you want to knock both of their heads together until you notice—there's water pouring from the ceiling in this apartment, too.

"Shut up, you two" you shout. "The water's coming from upstairs!"

"Stop changing the subject," your neighbor says. "Your parties really get out of hand. I'm not racist, but I think it's because of your loud Asian friend."

You don't even bother trying to calm your roommate's reaction. In fact, you kinda hope she kicks him in the balls. But still—

"Look," you say. "You're a shithead. But we have to stop the water upstairs."

"What—you're on his side now?" your roommate says, throwing her sponge at you.

"Fuck!" you scream at them both, and run out.

You climb the stairs more slowly this time—the adrenaline has left your system, you feel exhausted. And you really don't want to deal with this anymore.

You knock on the door anyway.

No one answers, so you knock again. You can hear running water, but no other sounds, no sloshing footsteps across carpet, nothing.

"There's... there's a flood," you stutter, knocking again.

The door finally opens, and the rich dude who lives there looks at you. You look at him and see he's dry, and there's no water on his floors.

"Our apartments are flooding" you tell him.

He nods, gives you a condescending look. "That's what you're all shouting about, huh?"

"It's coming from your apartment."

He shrugs his shoulders. "Oh, yeah. A pipe burst in my bathroom last night. But it's only flooding into the wall, so it's no big deal." He actually smiles at you when he says this.

"You have to turn off the water" you shout. "You're flooding the entire building."

"No I don't. But I'll sell you my mop if you need it."

"What?" You scream, starting to push past him.

He pushed you back, hard. "You poor people think you can just get stuff for free."

"I said turn off the water now, or I'll make you."

He looks behind you and smiles. You can hear what he hears echoing up from the other apartments—the sounds of your roommate and neighbor fighting. Beyond them you hear your other roommate crying, wringing out a wet towel, and you can even hear the old people on the first floor shouting.

"You and what army?" he laughs, pushing you out the door, slamming it in your face.

The world is flooding.

Literally: oceans are rising, land is disappearing, islands, villages, towns and cities are drowning. Climate change caused by human economic activity is killing people, causing wars, and slaughtering species. Governments and the rich have begun investing in special security measures for the coming chaos Capitalism has caused, while international climate change agreements still pretend minor changes to the way we distribute resources and pollute the earth will fix things.

We humans—the only ones who can actually stop what's happening—are staring at a nightmare scenario. Everything is going to shit: food shortages, resource wars, increasing poverty, heat waves, super storms. Cities choked with toxic fumes, massive deforestation, spreading deserts.

But we humans can't stop it until the tap is turned off, and no one can do that alone.

Just as in the flooded apartment, stopping the source of water won't replace the ruined books or furniture or anything else it destroyed—ending Capitalism alone won't fix the world. Turning off that tap—stopping Capitalism's relentless destruction—isn't going to undo any of that damage, just as overthrowing Capitalism won't magically stop racism, sexism, colonialism, or any other oppression under which we suffer.

Every single one of those things is a problem. Every single oppression, every single injustice, every single crisis—these things certainly matter. But none of these things can be resolved until the arrogant assholes above us, the rich, the politicians, all those who make sure the destruction continues, are dealt with first.

Sometimes when we talk about fighting Capitalism, people ask how we intend to stop racism and misogyny, transphobia and oppression of the disabled. Sometimes they even suggest those things are more important because they are more urgent. Sometimes people insist that any revolutionary movement must do all of those things at once, or it isn't revolutionary.

We can do all of those things. We should do all of those things. We must do all of those things.

But only one of those things has the power to affect every single person, destroy every life and make every person suffer. White and Black, First Nation and Asian, European and African, male and female, trans and cis, abled and disabled—each suffers under this thing.

It also affects the rest of the living world, the non-human beings upon which we rely for our very ability to survive. Mass extinction events, poisoned streams and lakes and oceans, soil that can no longer sustain life let alone food production, all the damage done by this one thing.

That thing is Capitalism.

By Capitalism though I don't mean a nebulous, undefined system. I mean the Capitalists, the living humans with names and addresses who make sure this damage happens because that's how they make their money. I mean the corporations who rip apart the earth to get at coal and petroleum to sell back to us, who tear down forests and poison rivers because it makes them money. And I mean the politicians who make sure no one challenges them, and the police and military paid to shoot anyone who wants this to stop.

That's not a lot of people, actually. But they have all the wealth and all the guns and all the media at their disposal. We only have us, our bodies, our creativity, our desire. But there are billions of us.

We are myriad, and they are few. But we forget this, forget the power we have. We forget this when we believe what they tell us, when we accept their narrative, when we let them terrify us.

We also forget this when we decide they are not the primary problem. We forget this when we decide people in the middle of the chain between us and them are actually the problem instead. We forget this when we insist fighting one group in the same situation is more important because they don't have it as bad as we do. We forget this when we decide the imperfect people around us are too imperfect to fight alongside.

Revolution will not save the world. The overthrow of Capitalism won't solve every problem in front of us. There will still be idiots and oppressive jerks, there will still be violence against women and disabled people, there will still be racists and transphobes.

But what there won't be is Capitalism.

There won't be a system that lets some people have everything and forces the rest of us to fight amongst ourselves for what's left. There won't be a system making sure the earth is destroyed so a small handful of people can live like kings and queens.

We can have this, but never will if we insist that other problems are more important. We can have this, but never will if we wait for perfect allies who never oppress anyone. And we can have this, but never will if we don't do something soon.

The world is flooding, and we know why.

Let's stop it.

# RHYD WILDERMUTH

is the co-founder of Gods&Radicals. He is a theorist,
Pagan, punk, poet, and currently lives in Bretagne.

# GODS&RADICALS PRESS

is a not-for-profit Pagan anti-capitalist publisher.
For more information about our works, visit our websites:
ABEAUTIFULRESISTANCE.ORG
GODSANDRADICALS.ORG